# TODAY'S GREATEST
# Pop & Rock Hits

**BIG NOTE PIANO**

Arranged by
Carol Matz

Produced by
Alfred Music Publishing Co., Inc.
P.O. Box 10003
Van Nuys, CA 91410-0003
alfred.com

Printed in USA.

ISBN-10: 0-7390-9480-7
ISBN-13: 978-0-7390-9480-8

# 21 GUNS

Words and Music by
Billie Joe, Green Day,
David Bowie, and John Phillips
Arranged by Carol Matz

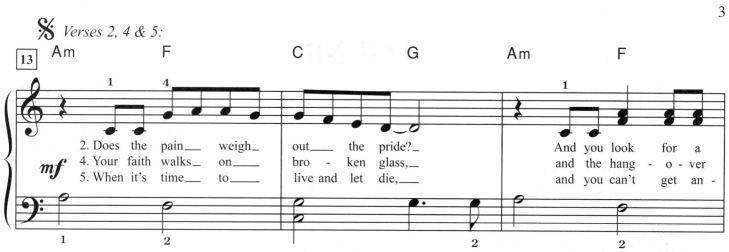
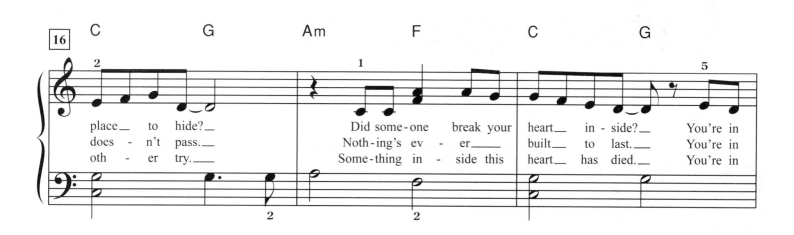
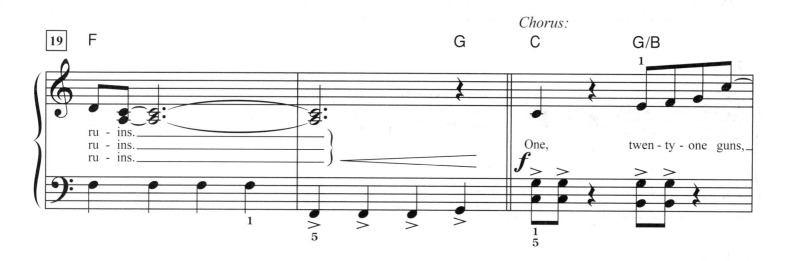

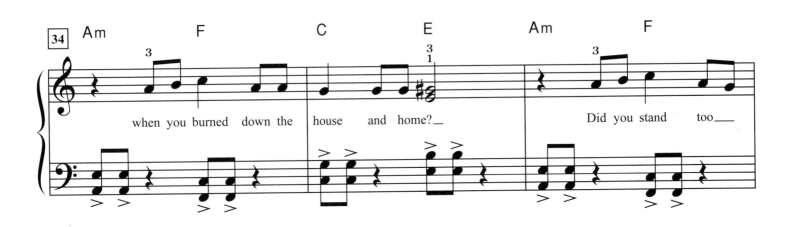

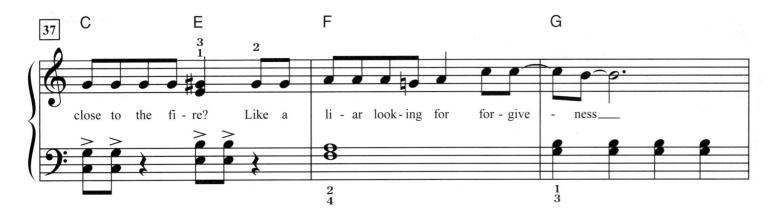

close to the fi - re? Like a li - ar look-ing for for-give - ness____

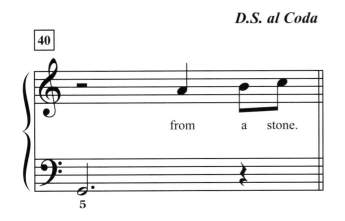

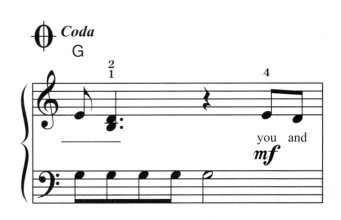

*D.S. al Coda*

*Coda*

from a stone.

you and

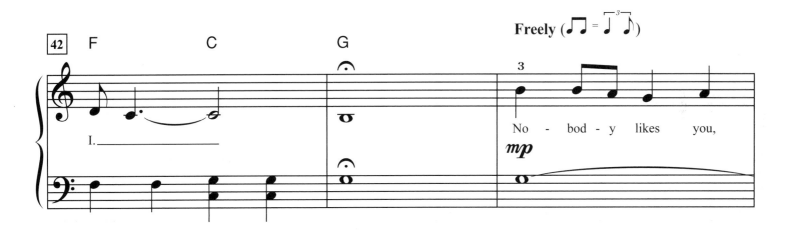

**Freely**

I.____

No - bod - y likes you,

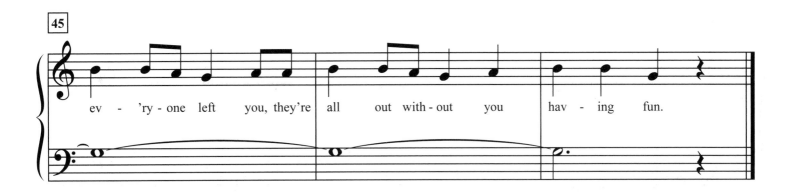

ev - 'ry - one left you, they're all out with - out you hav - ing fun.

# ALL-AMERICAN GIRL

Words and Music by Carrie Underwood,
Kellie Lovelace and Ashley Gorley
Arranged by Carol Matz

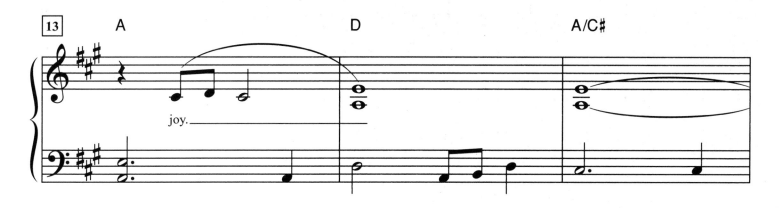

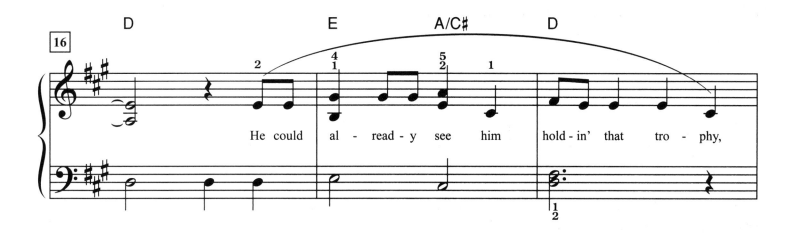

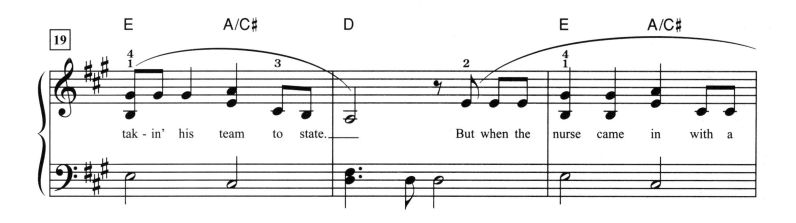

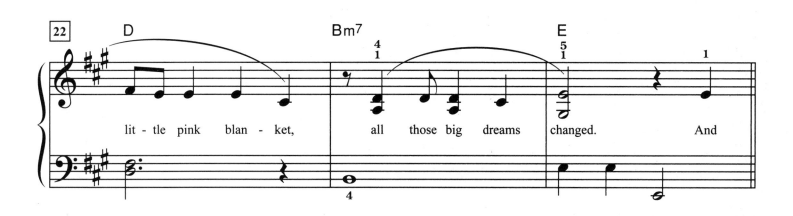

7

8

*Chorus:*

now he's wrapped— a-round her fin-ger. She's the cen-ter of___ his whole world.___

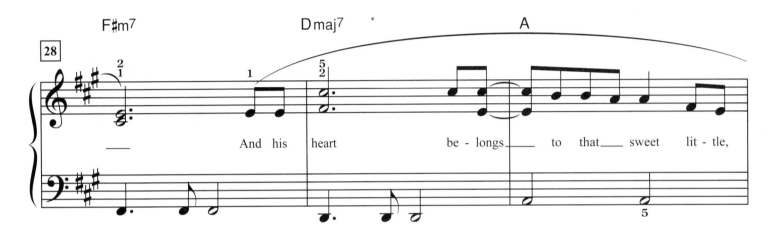

___ And his heart be-longs___ to that___ sweet lit-tle,

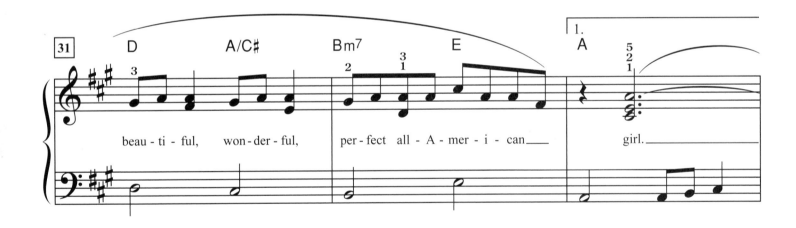

beau-ti-ful, won-der-ful, per-fect all-A-mer-i-can___ girl.___

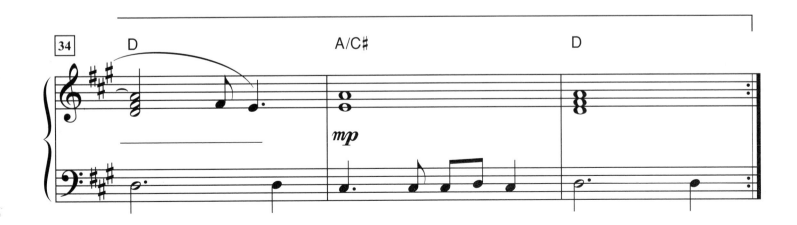

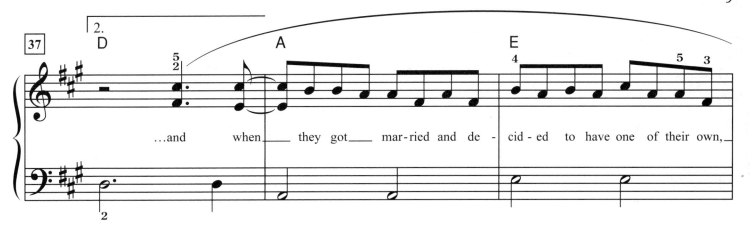

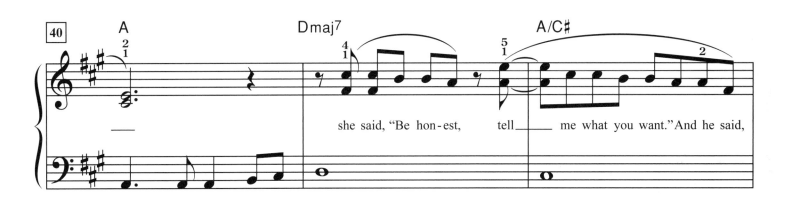

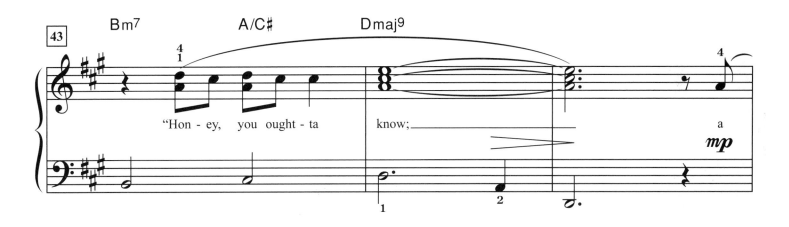

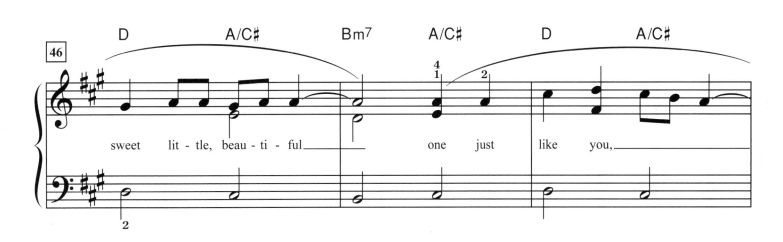

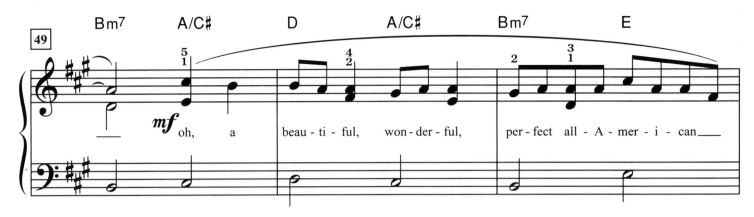

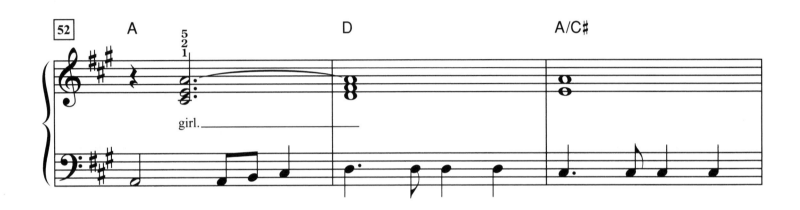

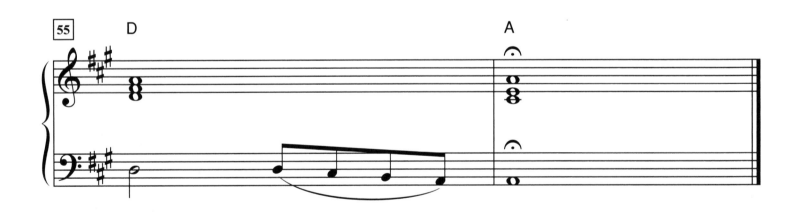

*Verse 2:*
Sixteen short years later,
she was falling for the senior football star.
Before you knew it he was droppin' passes,
skippin' practice just to spend more time with her.
The coach said, "Hey son, what's your problem?
Tell me, have you lost your mind?"
Daddy said, "You'll lose your free ride to college.
Boy, you better tell her goodbye." But…
*(Chorus)*

# THE BIG BANG THEORY (MAIN TITLE)

Words and Music by
Ed Robertson
Arranged by Carol Matz

# BABY

Words and Music by Terius Nash, Christopher Stewart,
Christine Flores, Christopher Bridges and Justin Bieber
Arranged by Carol Matz

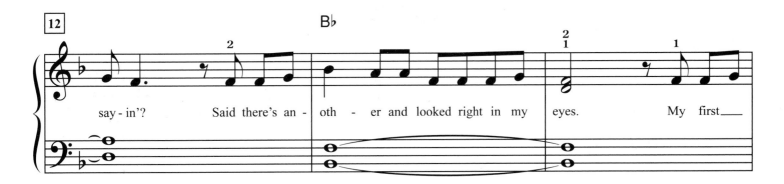

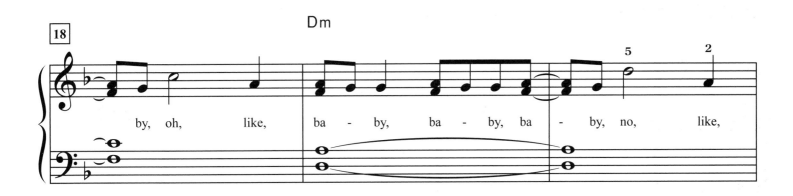

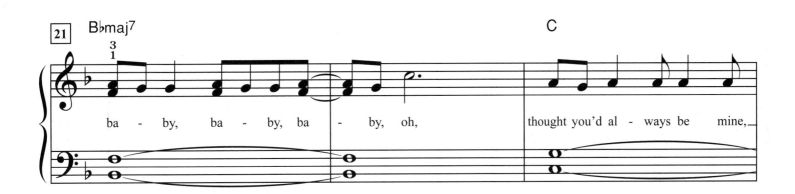

14

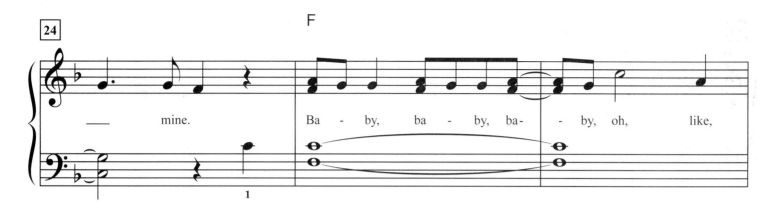

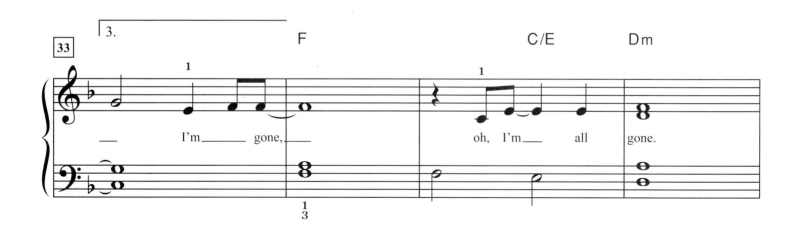

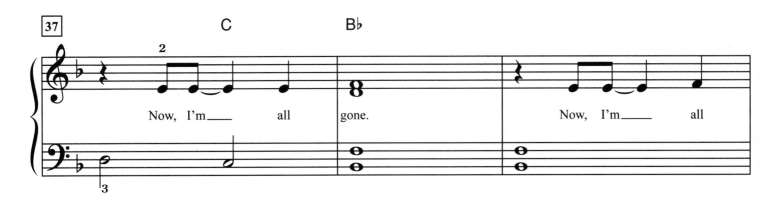

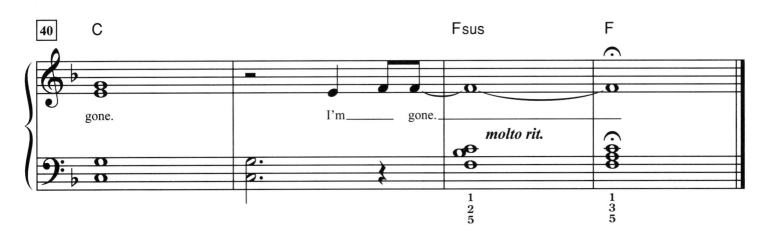

*Verse 2:*
Oh, for you, I would've done whatever,
And I just can't believe we ain't together.
And I wanna play it cool, but I'm losing you.
I'll buy you anything. I'll buy you any ring.
And I'm in pieces, baby, fix me.
And just shake me till you wake me from this bad dream.
I'm going down, down, down, down.
And I just can't believe my first love won't be around
And I'm like...
*(To Chorus:)*

*Verse 3 Rap:*
Luda!
When I was thirteen, I had my first love.
There was nobody that compared to my baby.
And nobody came between us,
Or could ever come above.
She had me going crazy,
Oh, I was starstruck.
She woke me up daily,
Don't need no Starbucks.
She made my heart pound
And skip a beat when I see her in the street,
And at school, on the playground.
But I really wanna see her on a weekend.
She knows she got me dazing,
'Cause she was so amazing.
And now, my heart is breakin',
But I just keep on sayin'...
*(To Chorus:)*

# BORN TO BE SOMEBODY

Words and Music by Diane Warren
Arranged by Carol Matz

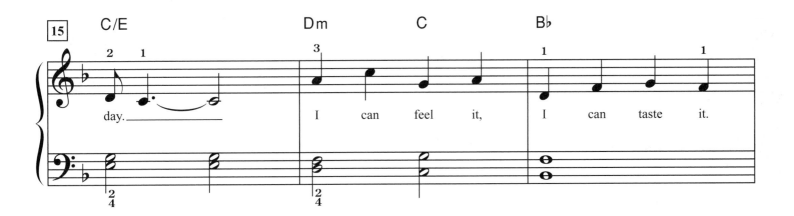

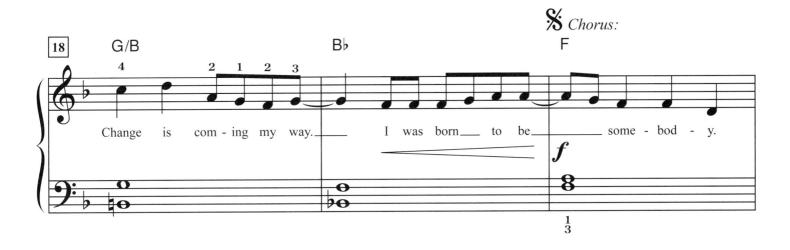

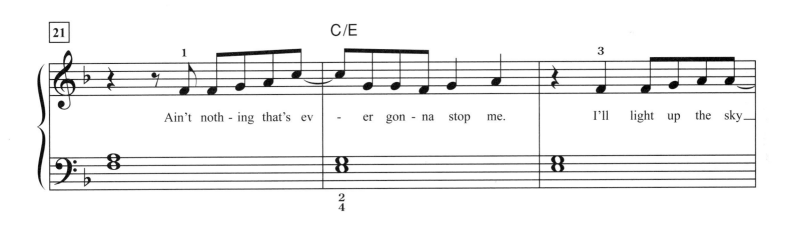

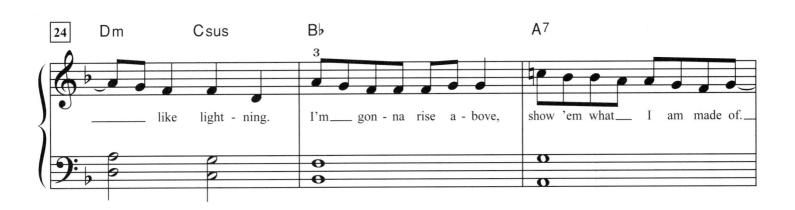

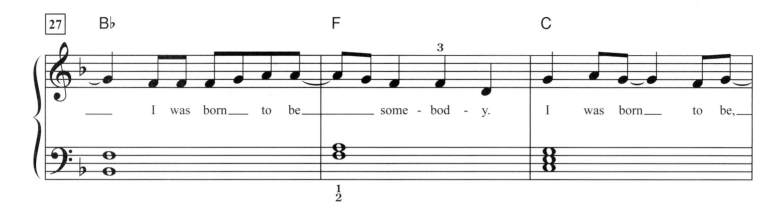

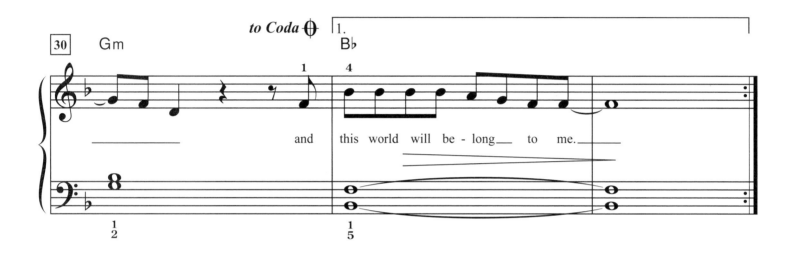

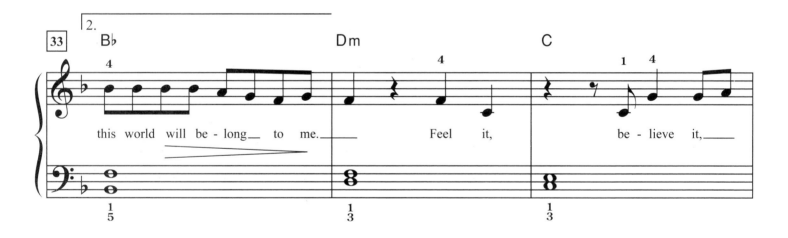

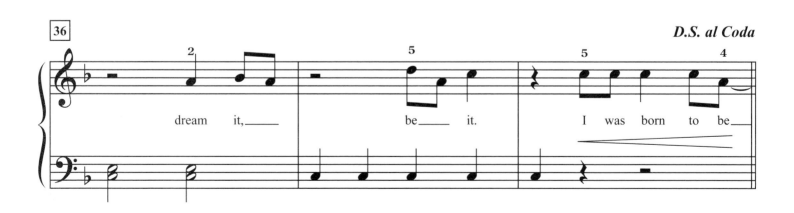

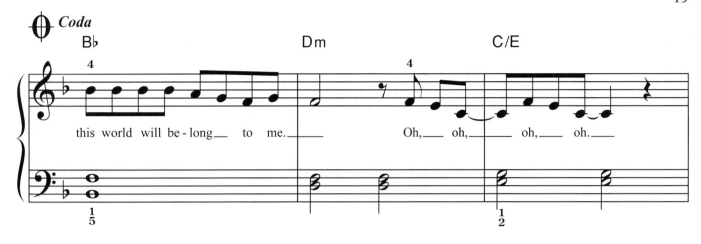

*Verse 2:*
This life can kick you around.
This world can make you feel small.
But they will not keep me down.
I was born to stand tall.
I'm going all the way.
I can feel it, I believe it.
I'm here, I'm here to stay.
*(To Chorus:)*

# BOYFRIEND

Words and Music by
Mason Levy, Matthew Tyler Musto,
Mike Posner and Justin Bieber
Arranged by Carol Matz

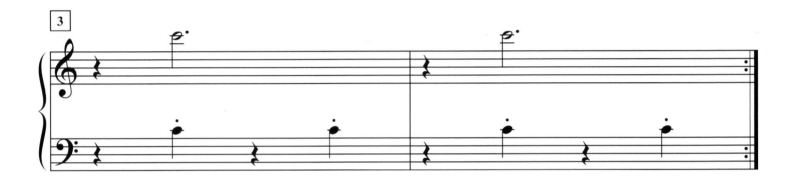

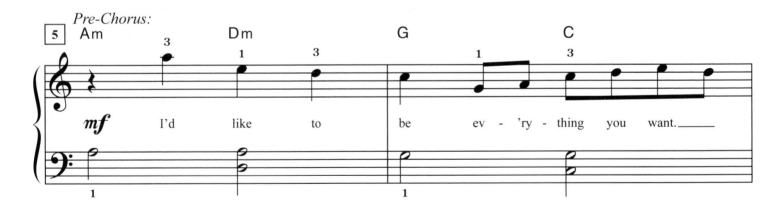

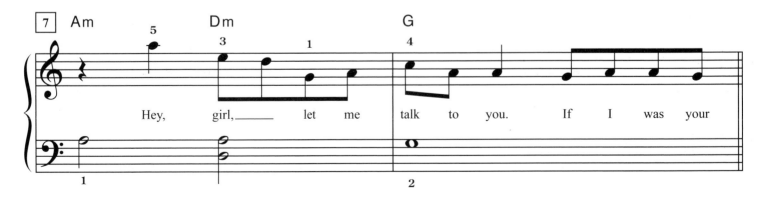

*Chorus:*

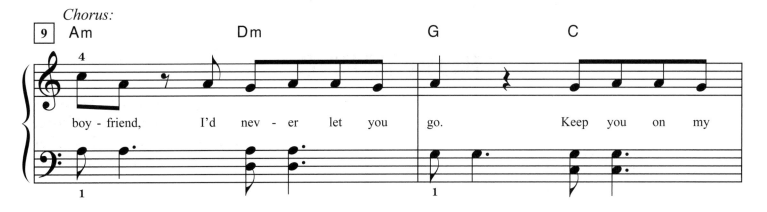

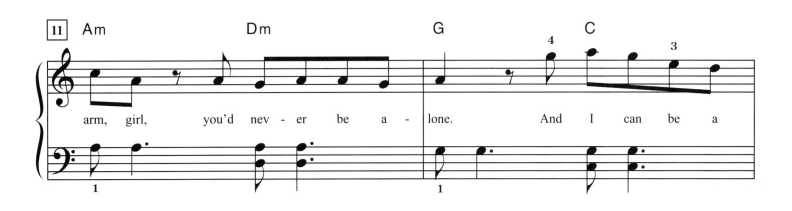

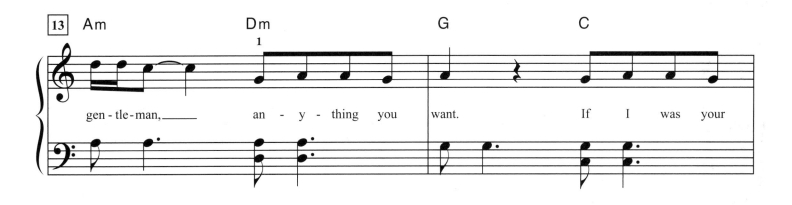

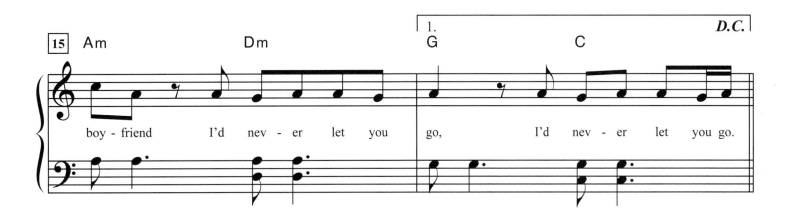

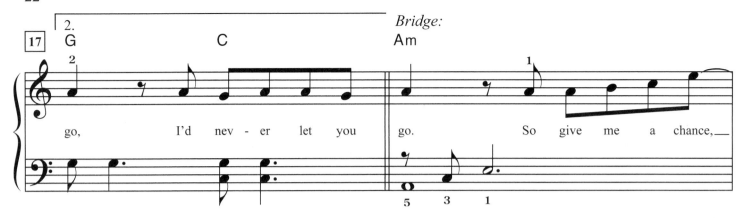

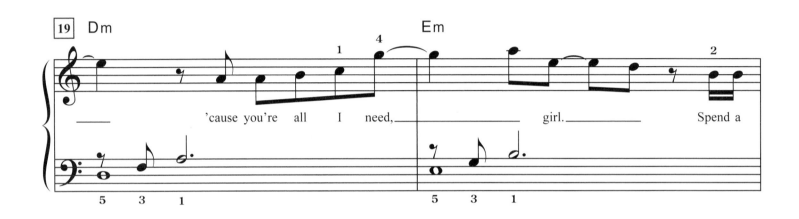

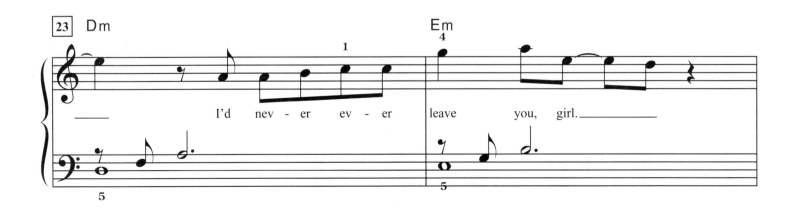

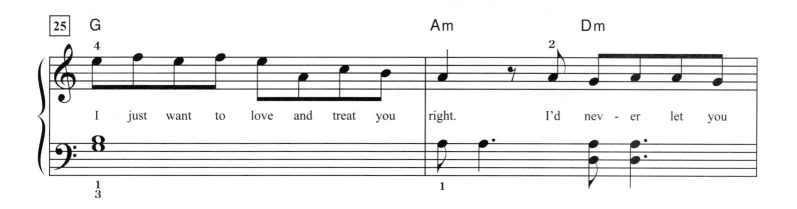

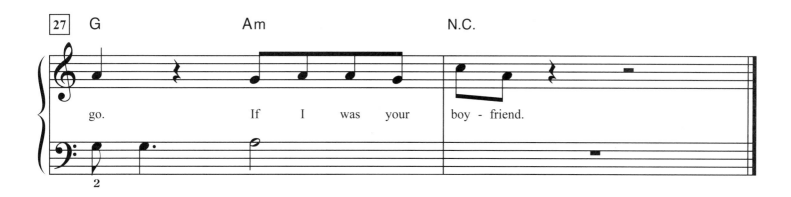

Verse 1 (rap):
*If I was your boyfriend, I'd never let you go.*
*I can take you places you ain't never been before.*
*Baby, take a chance or you'll never ever know.*
*I got money in my hands that I'd really like to blow,*
*Swag, swag, swag, on you.*
*Chillin' by the fire while we eatin' fondue,*
*I don't know about me but I know about you.*
*So say hello to falsetto in three, two, swag.*

Verse 2 (rap):
*Tell me what you like, yeah, tell me what you don't.*
*I could be your Buzz Lightyear, fly across the globe.*
*I don't never wanna fight; yeah, you already know.*
*Imma make you shine bright like you're laying in the snow, brrr.*
*Girlfriend, girlfriend, you could be my girlfriend,*
*You could be my girlfriend until the world ends.*
*Make you dance, do a spin and a twirl, and*
*Voice goin' crazy on this hook like a whirlwind, swaggie.*

# BILLIONAIRE

Words and Music by
Peter Hernandez, Philip Lawrence,
Ari Levine and Travis McCoy
Arranged by Carol Matz

**Moderate reggae**

*Chorus:*

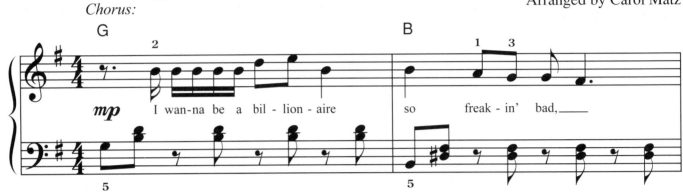

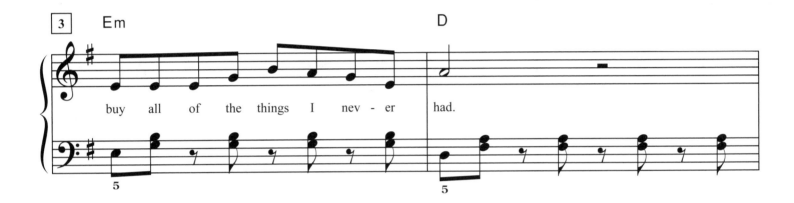

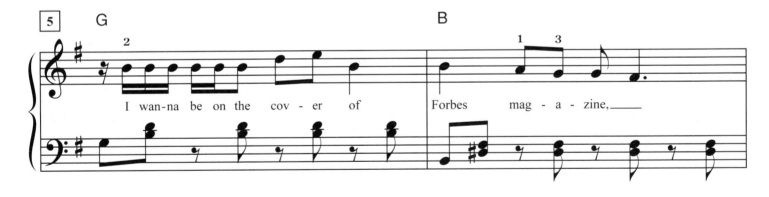

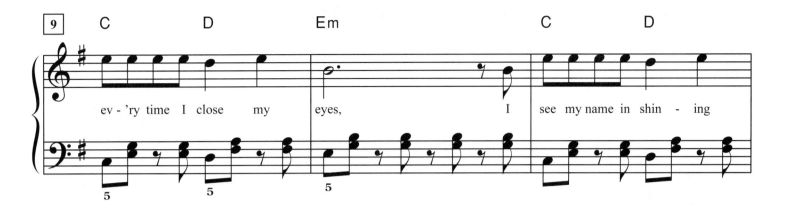

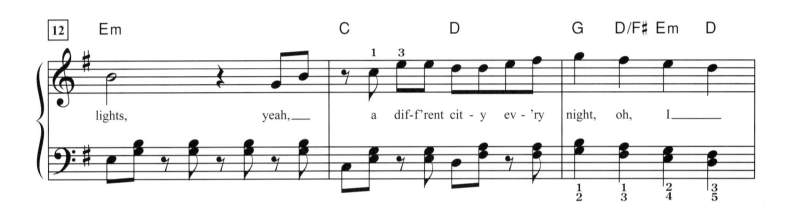

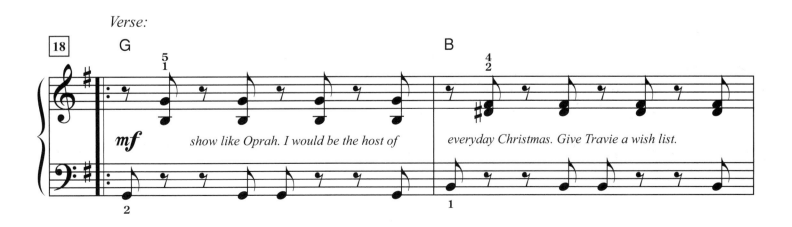

*Bridge:*

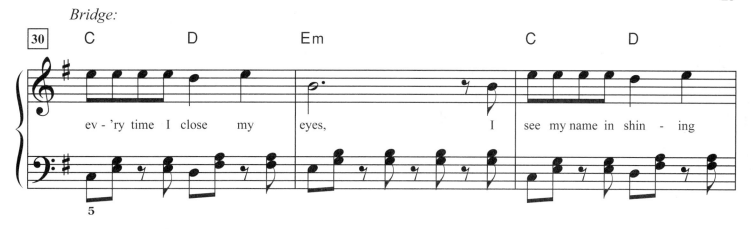

**30** C D Em C D

ev - 'ry time I close my eyes, I see my name in shin - ing

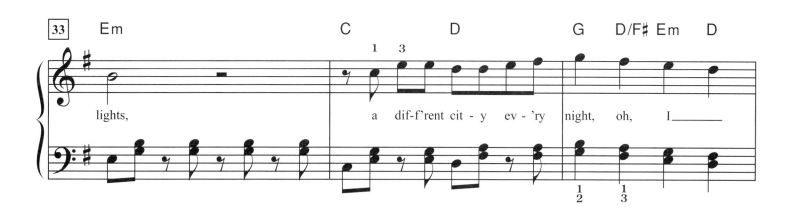

**33** Em C D G D/F♯ Em D

lights, a dif-f'rent cit - y ev - 'ry night, oh, I\_\_\_\_

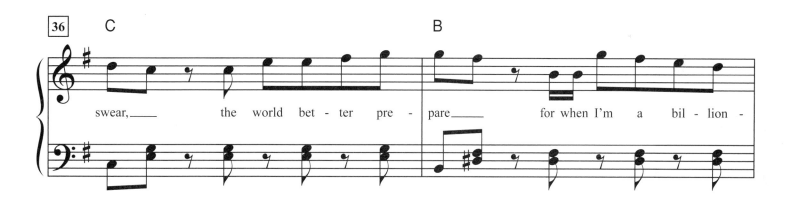

**36** C B

swear,\_\_\_\_ the world bet - ter pre - pare\_\_\_\_ for when I'm a bil - lion -

**38** Em Am Em

aire. Oh,\_\_\_\_ oh,\_\_\_\_ when I'm a bil - lion - aire. Oh,\_\_\_\_ oh.

2. See additional lyrics.

*Verse 2:*
*(Rap)*
*I'll be playing basketball with the President*
*Dunking on his delegates,*
*Then I'll compliment him on his political etiquette,*
*Toss a couple milli in the air just for the heck of it,*
*But keep the fives, twenties, tens, and Bens completely separate.*
*Yeah, I'll be in a whole new tax bracket.*
*We in a recession, but let me take a crack at it.*
*I'll probably take whatever's left and just split it up,*
*So everybody that I love can have a couple bucks.*
*And not a single tummy around me*
*Would know what hungry was, eating good, sleeping soundly.*
*I know we all have a similar dream.*
*Go in your pocket, pull out your wallet, put it in the air and sing.*

# CALIFORNIA GURLS

Words and Music by Katy Perry, Lukasz Gottwald, Max
Martin, Bonnie Mckee, Benjamin Levin and Calvin Broadus
Arranged by Carol Matz

**Moderately fast**
*Verses:*

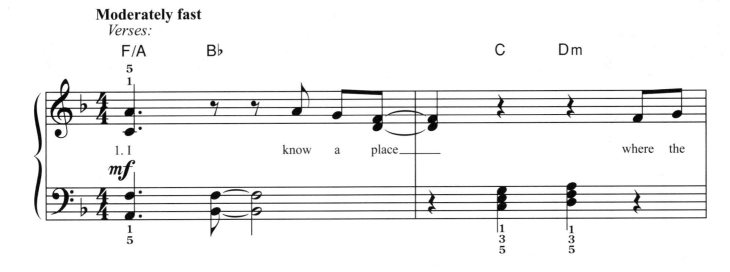

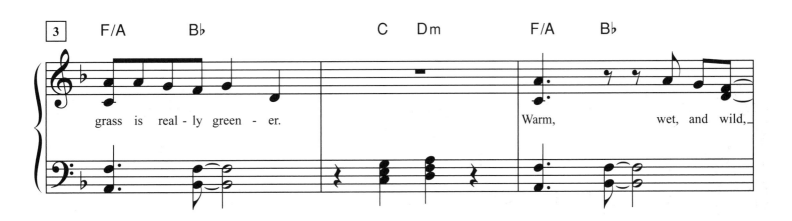

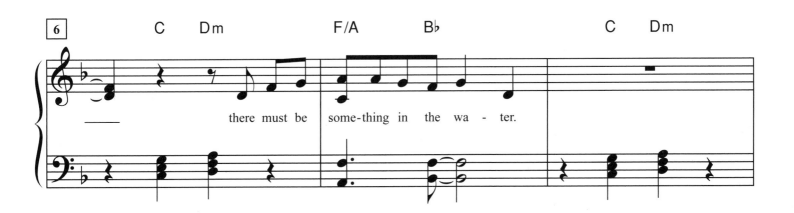

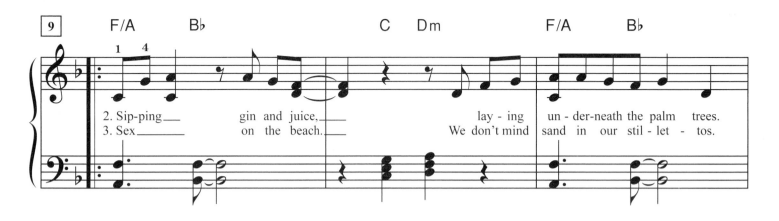

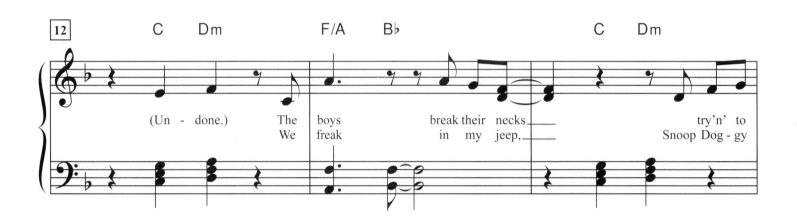

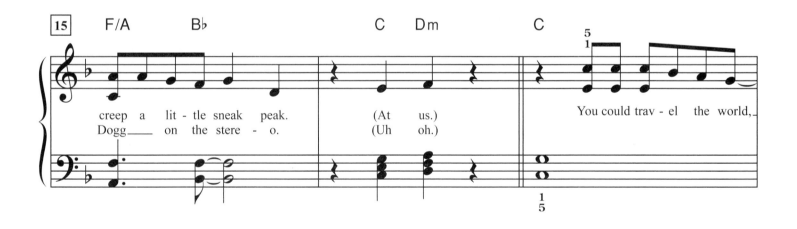

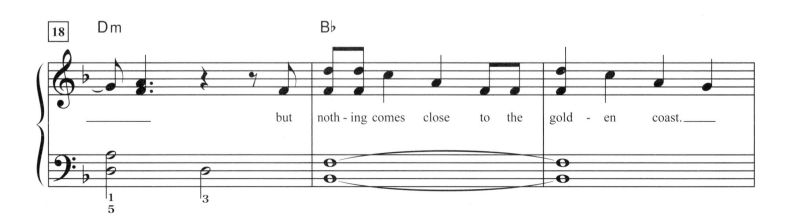

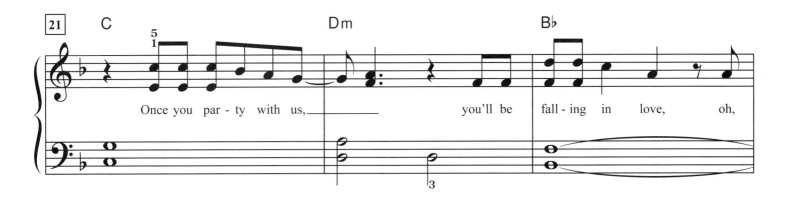

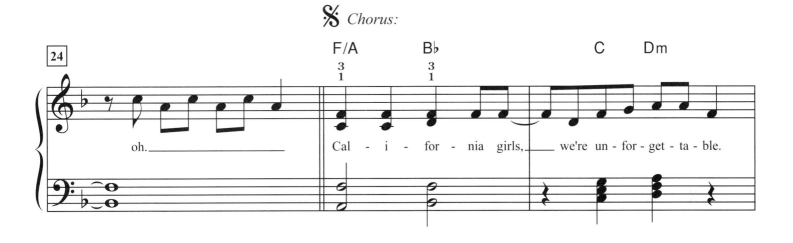

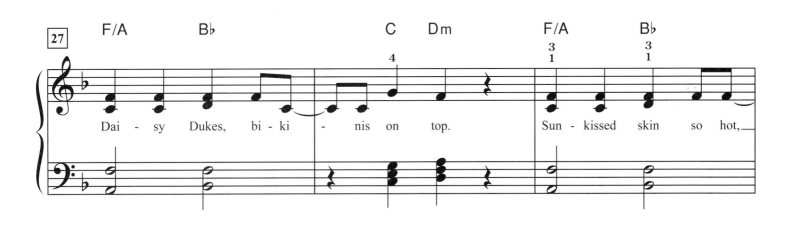

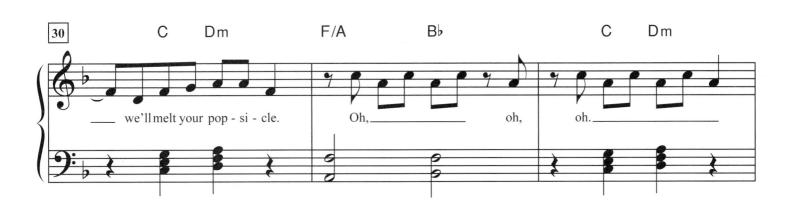

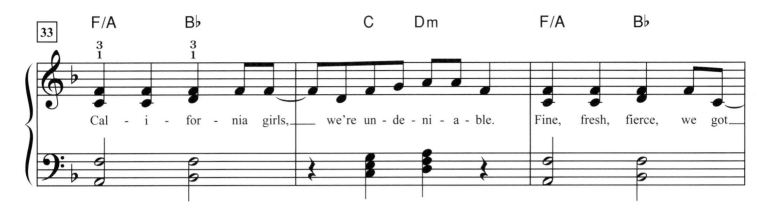

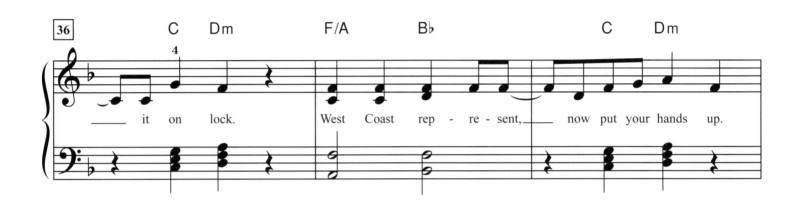

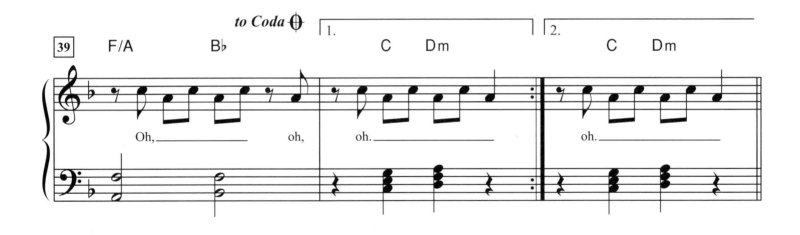

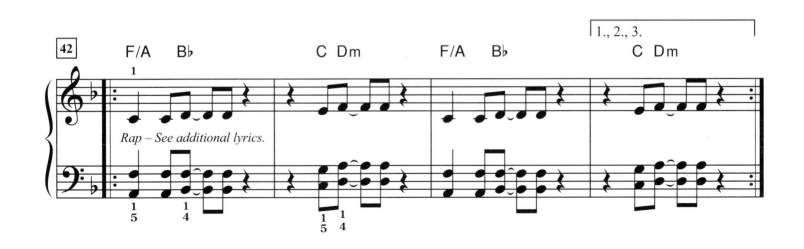

*Rap:*
*Tone, tan, fit and ready.*
*Turn it up 'cause it's gettin' heavy.*
*Wild, wild west coast,*
*These are the girls I love the most.*
*I mean the ones, I mean, like she's the one.*
*Kiss her, touch her, squeeze her buns.*

*The girl's a freak, she drive a jeep,*
*And live on the beach.*
*I'm okay, I won't play.*
*I love the bait, just like I love L.A.*
*Venice Beach and Palm Springs,*
*Summertime is everything.*

*Homeboys hanging out.*
*All that a\*\* hanging out.*
*Bikinis, zucchinis, martinis, no weenies.*
*Just a king and a queenie.*
*Katy, my lady. (Yeah.)*
*Ah, lookie here, baby. (Uh huh.)*
*I'm all up on you,*
*'Cause you're representin' California.*
*(To Chorus:)*

# COUGH SYRUP

Words and Music by
Sameer Gadhia, Eric Cannata, Jacob Tilley,
Francois Comtois and Ehson Hashemian
Arranged by Carol Matz

**Moderate rock**

*Verse:*

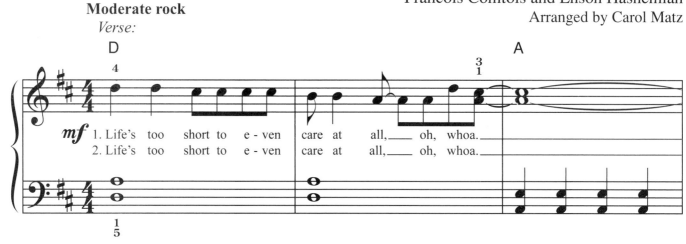

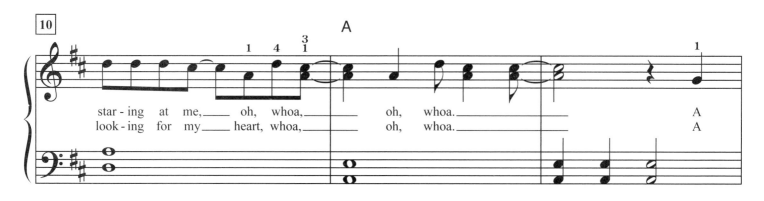

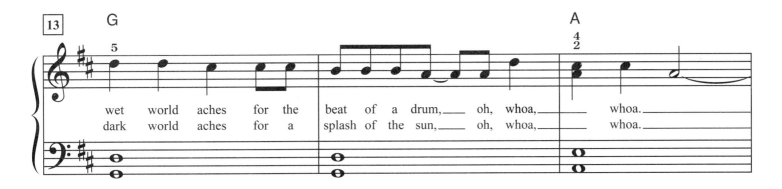

wet  world  aches  for  the  beat  of  a  drum,___ oh,  whoa,___ whoa.___
dark  world  aches  for  a  splash  of  the  sun,___ oh,  whoa,___ whoa.___

*Chorus:*

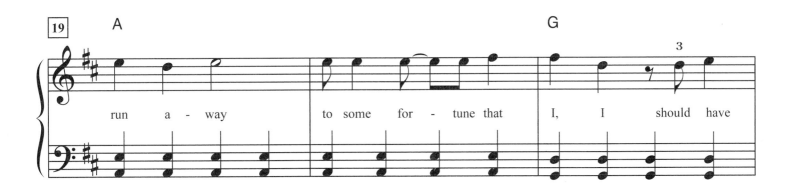

If  I  could  find  a  way  to  see___ this  straight,  I'd

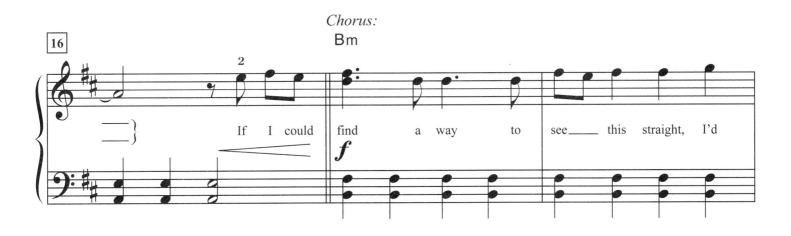

run  a - way  to  some  for - tune  that  I,  I  should  have

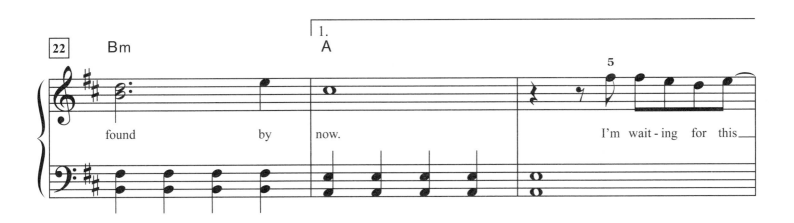

found  by  now.  I'm  wait - ing  for  this___

# DON'T STOP BELIEVIN'

Words and Music by
Jonathan Cain, Neal Schon and Steve Perry
Arranged by Carol Matz

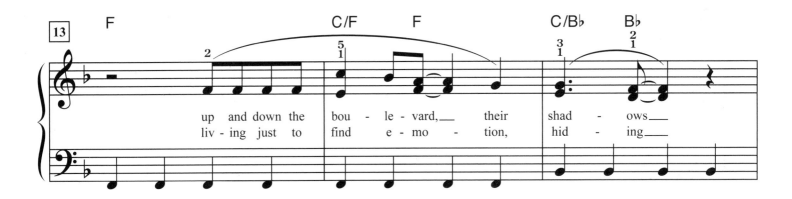

up and down the bou - le - vard,___ their shad - ows___
liv - ing just to find e - mo - tion, hid - ing___

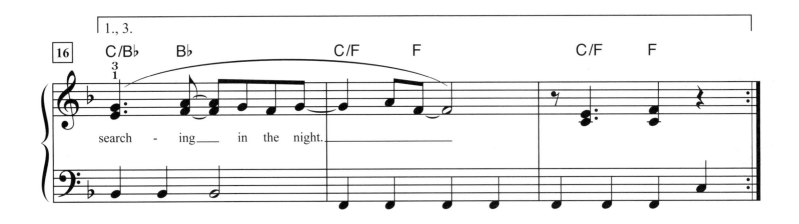

1., 3.

search - ing___ in the night.___

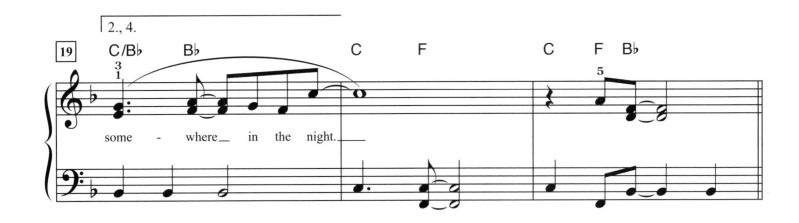

2., 4.

some - where___ in the night.___

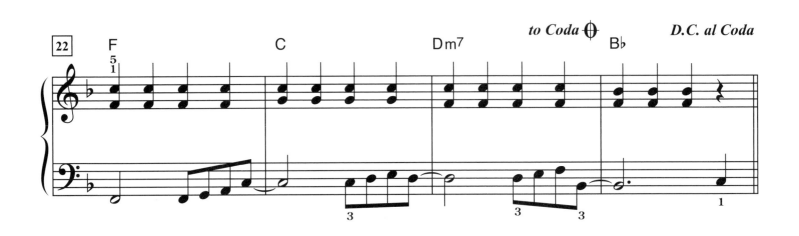

*to Coda* ⊕  *D.C. al Coda*

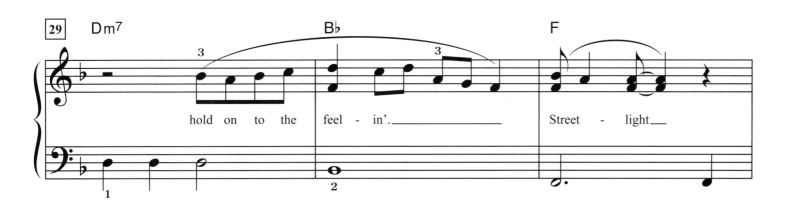

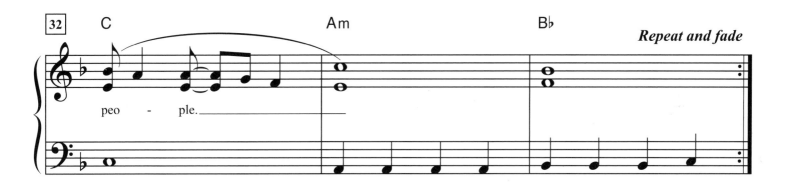

*Verse 3:*
A singer in a smoky room,
the smell of wine and cheap perfume.
For a smile they can share the night,
it goes on and on and on and on.

*Verse 4:*
Working hard to get my fill.
Everybody wants a thrill,
payin' anything to roll the dice
just one more time.

*Verse 5:*
Some will win and some will lose,
some were born to sing the blues.
Oh, the movie never ends,
it goes on and on and on and on.

# EVERYBODY TALKS

Words and Music by
Tyler Glenn and Tim Pagnotta
Arranged by Carol Matz

**Moderately fast**

*Verse:*

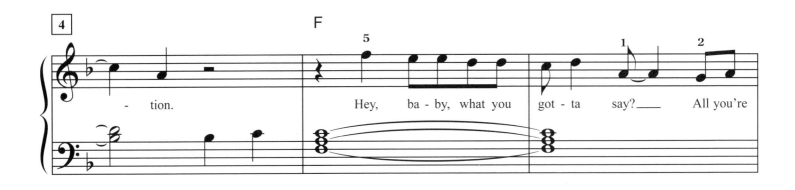

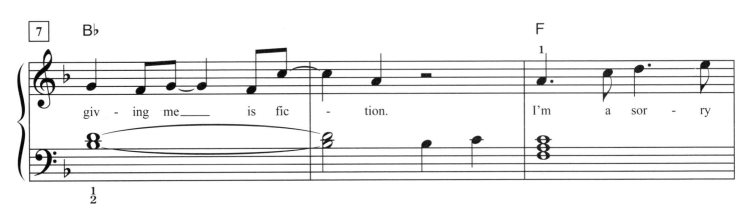

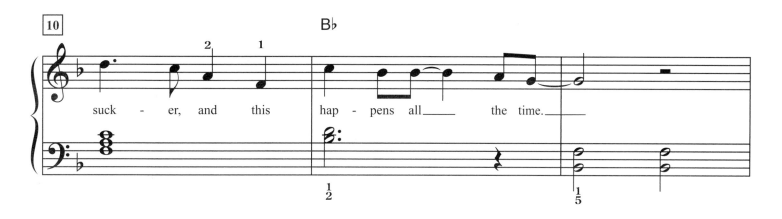

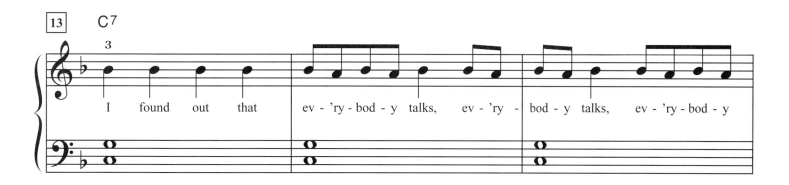

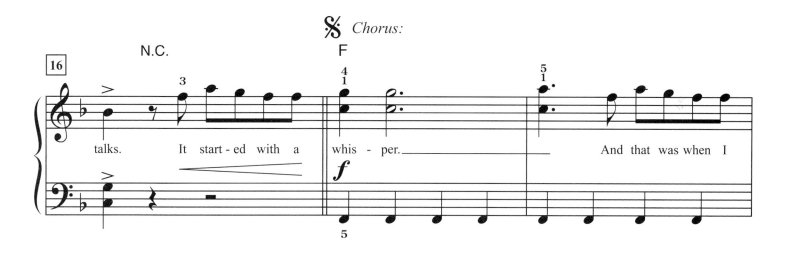

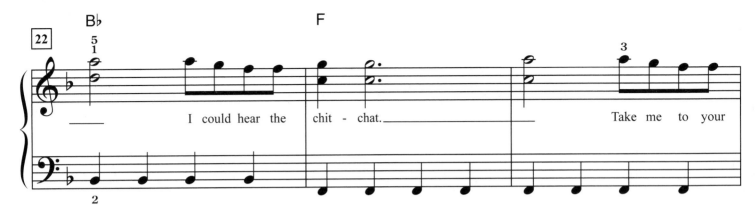

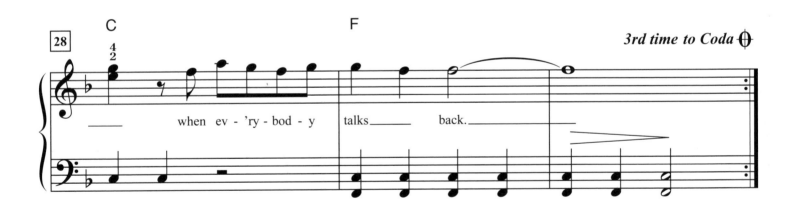

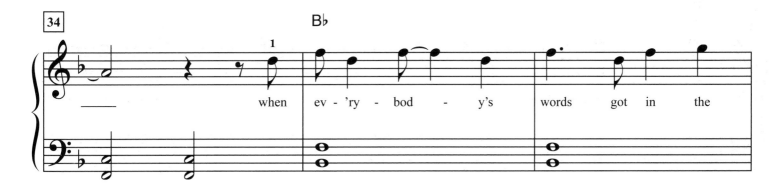

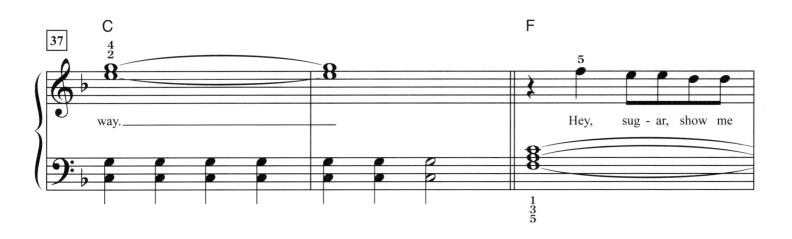

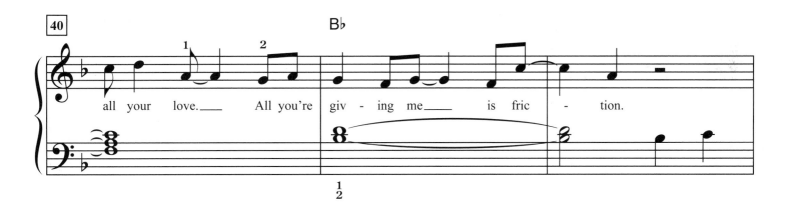

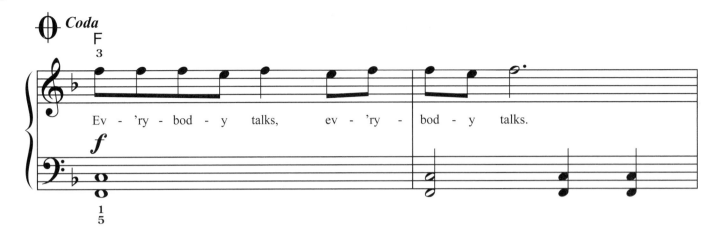

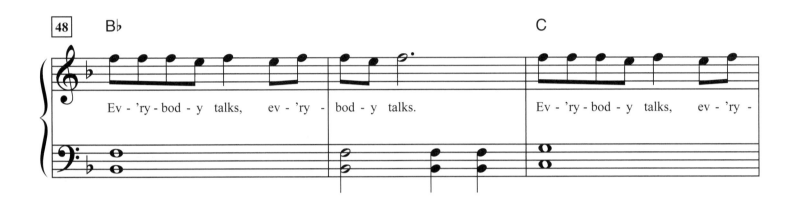

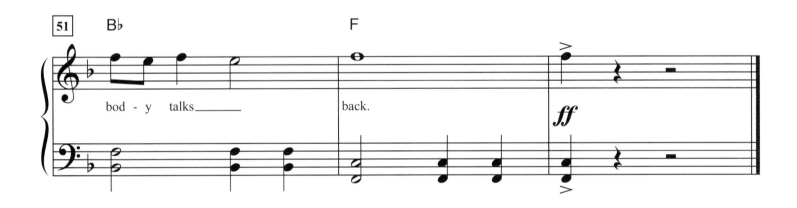

*Verse 2:*
Hey, honey, you could be my drug.
You could be my new prescription.
Too much could be an overdose.
All this trash talk make me itchin'.
Oh my my, everybody talks, everybody talks,
Everybody talks too much.
*(To Chorus:)*

# FIREWORK

Words and Music by
Katy Perry, Mikkel Eriksen, Tor Erik Hermansen,
Sandy Wilhelm and Ester Dean
Arranged by Carol Matz

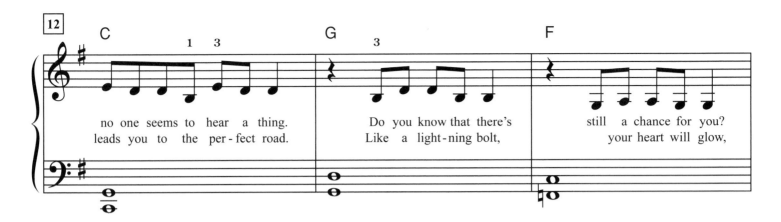

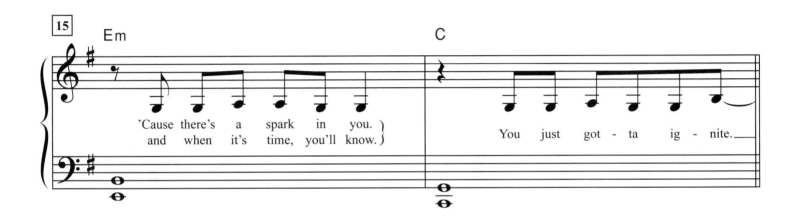

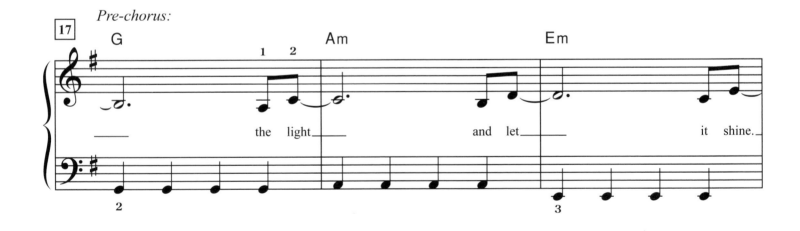

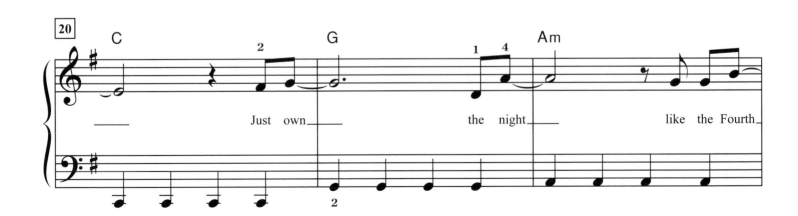

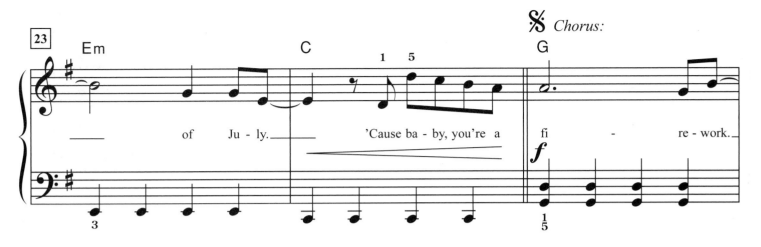

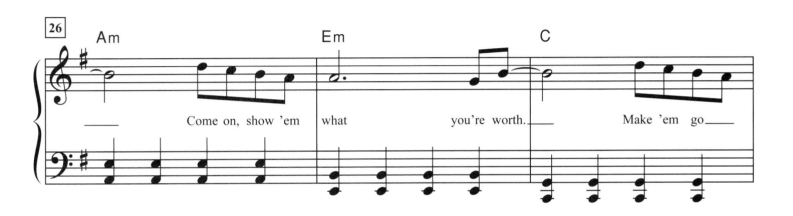

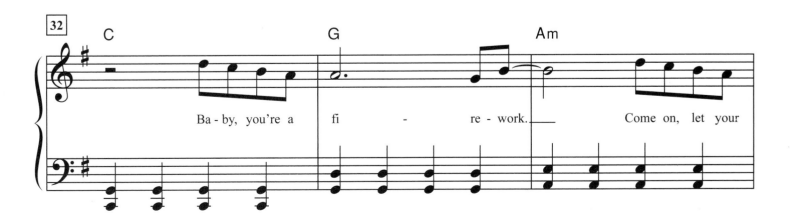

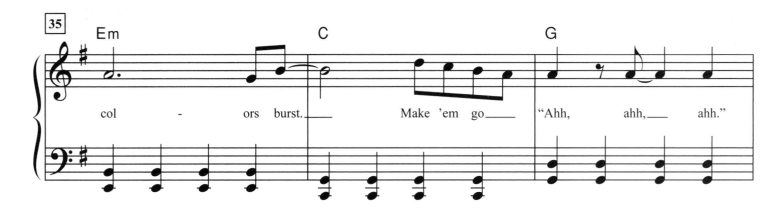

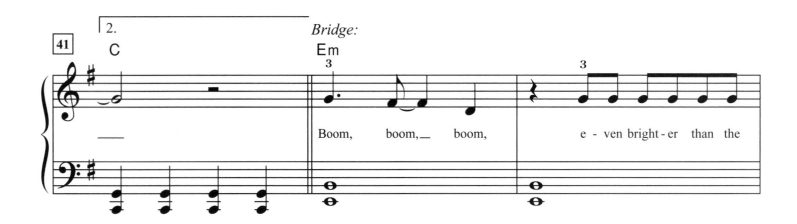

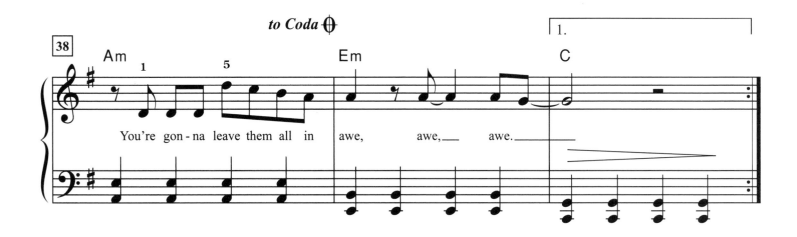

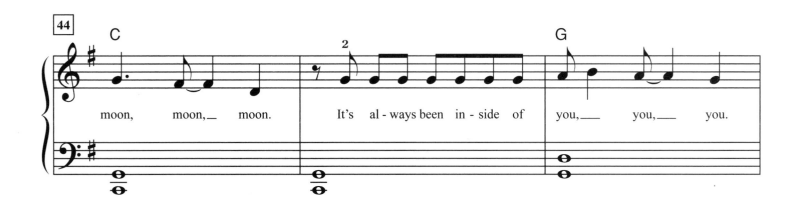

D.S. al Coda

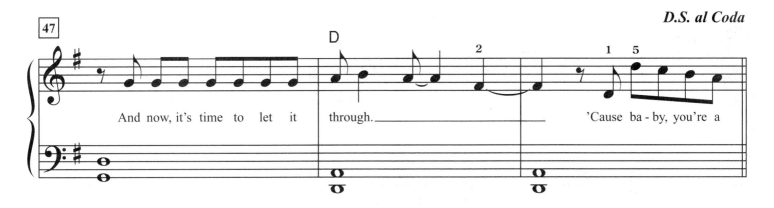

And now, it's time to let it through._____ 'Cause ba - by, you're a

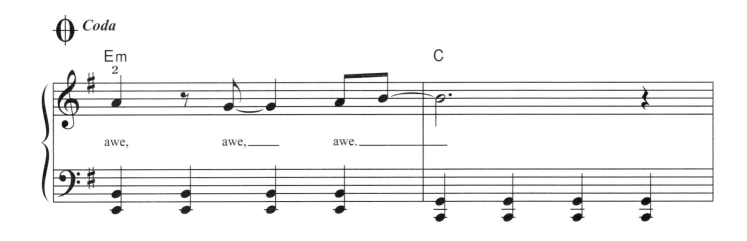

awe, awe,\_\_\_\_\_ awe.\_\_\_\_\_

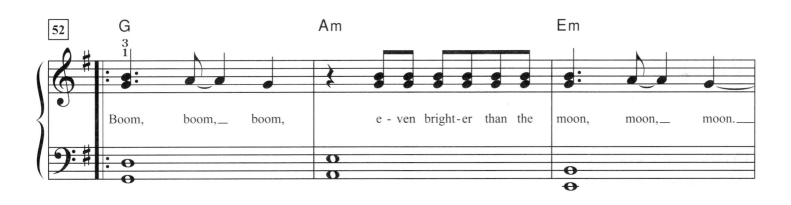

Boom, boom,\_ boom, e - ven bright-er than the moon, moon,\_ moon.

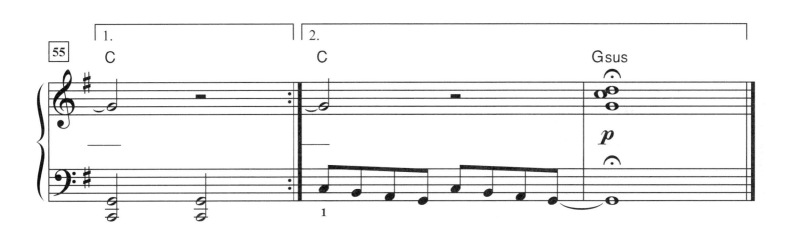

# FORGET YOU

Words and Music by
Christopher Brown, Peter Hernandez, Ari Levine,
Philip Lawrence and Thomas "Cee Lo" Callaway
Arranged by Carol Matz

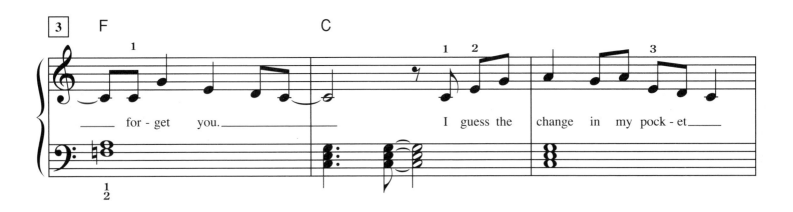

53

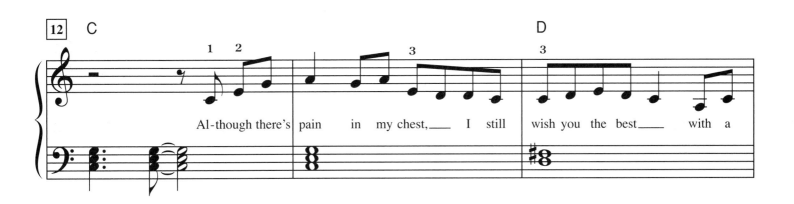

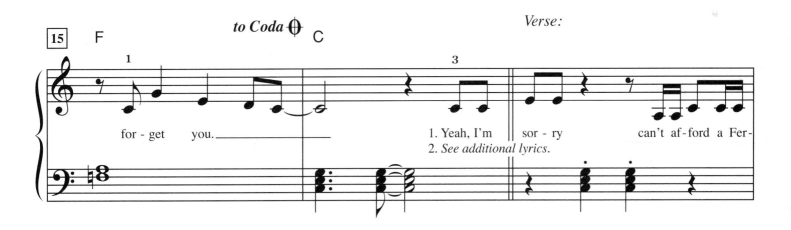

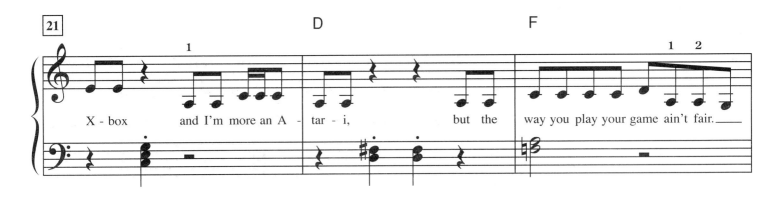

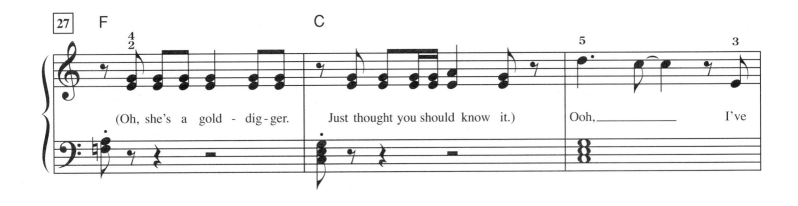

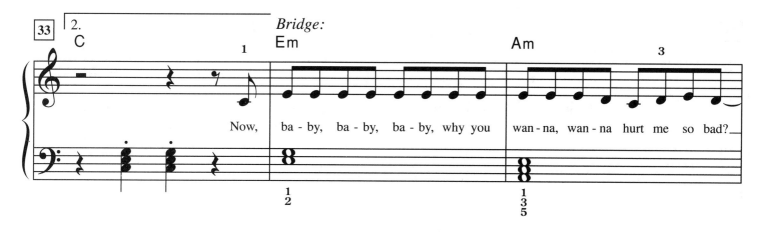

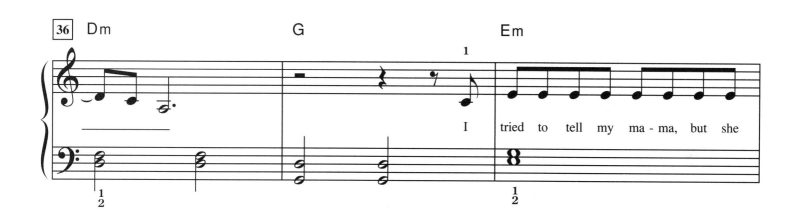

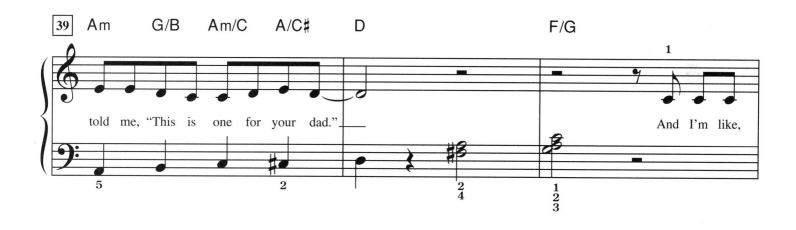

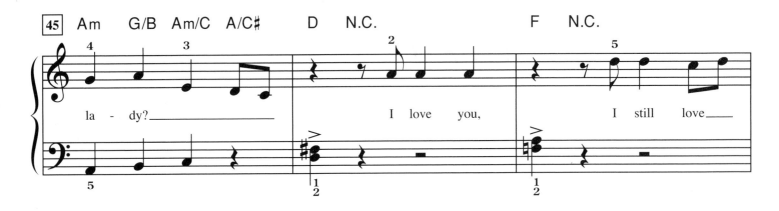

**45** Am G/B Am/C A/C♯ D N.C. F N.C.

la - dy?____ I love you, I still love____

**48** G

*D.S. al Coda*

you.____ Oh, I see you

*Coda*
C

*Verse 2:*
Now, I know that I had to borrow,
Beg and steal and lie and cheat,
Tryin' to keep ya, tryin' to please ya,
'Cause being in love with your a** ain't cheap.

# GLAD YOU CAME

Words and Music by
Edward Drewett, Wayne Hector and Steve Mac
Arranged by Carol Matz

**Freely**

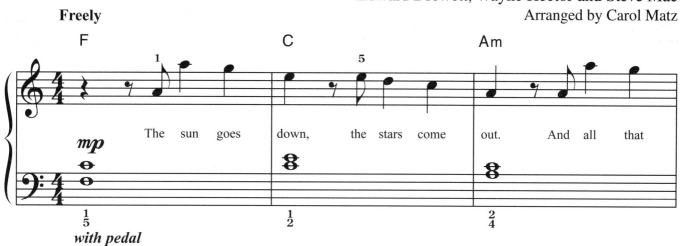

The sun goes down, the stars come out. And all that

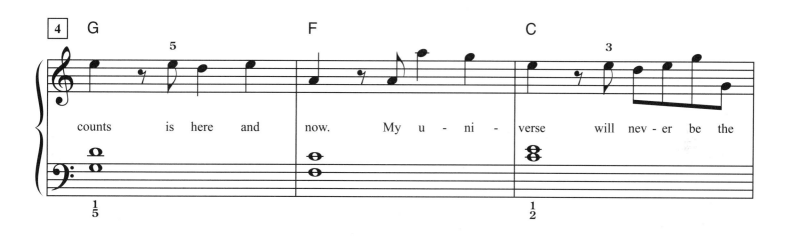

counts is here and now. My u - ni - verse will nev - er be the

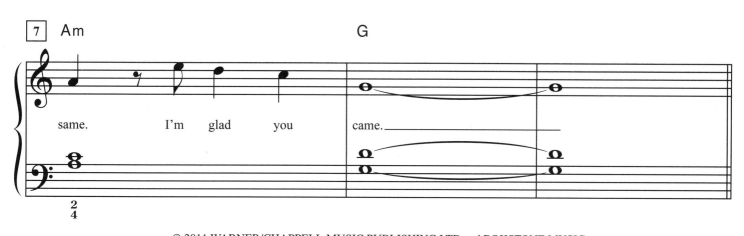

same. I'm glad you came.

**Moderately fast**

(no pedal)

*Verse:*

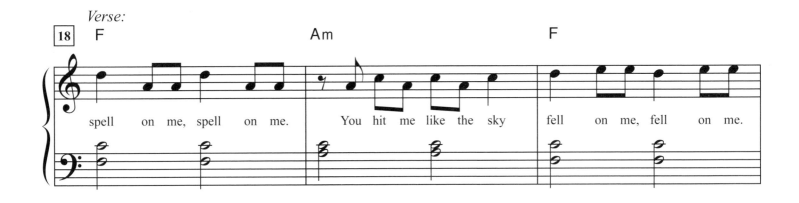

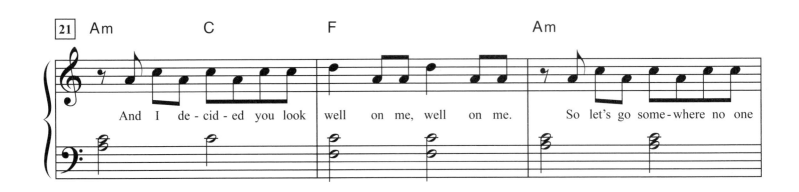

59

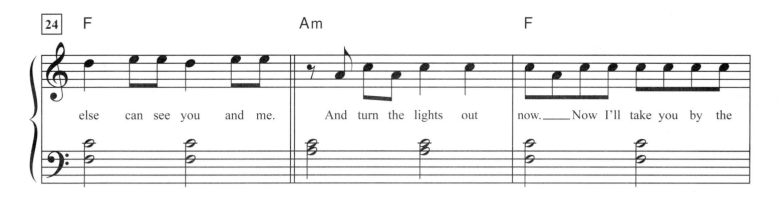

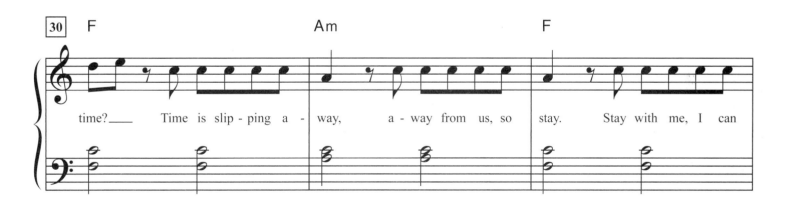

*Chorus:*

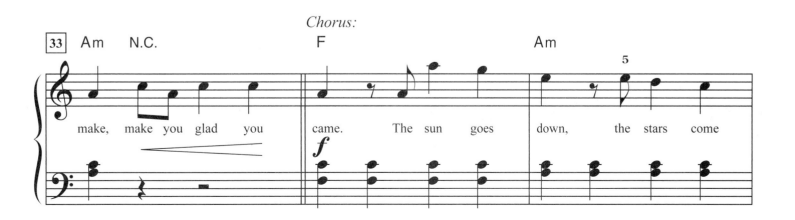

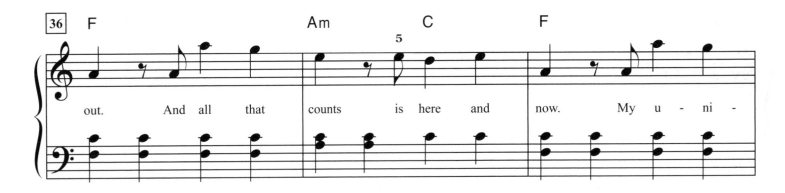

out. And all that counts is here and now. My u - ni -

verse will nev - er be the same. I'm glad you came. I'm glad you

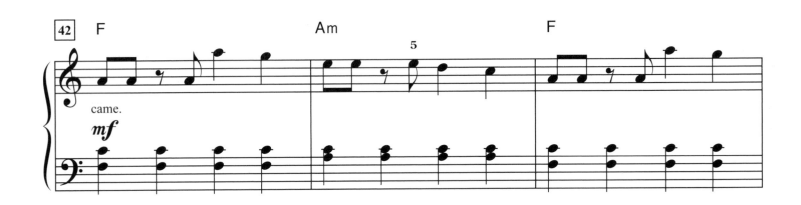

came.
*mf*

I'm glad you came.

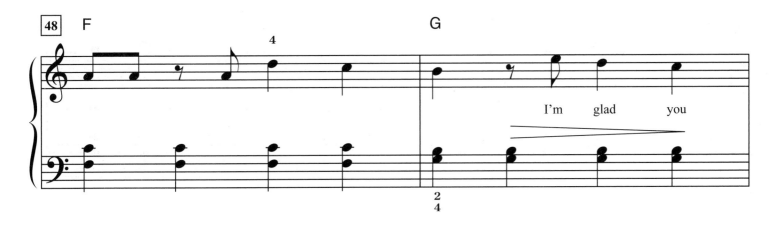

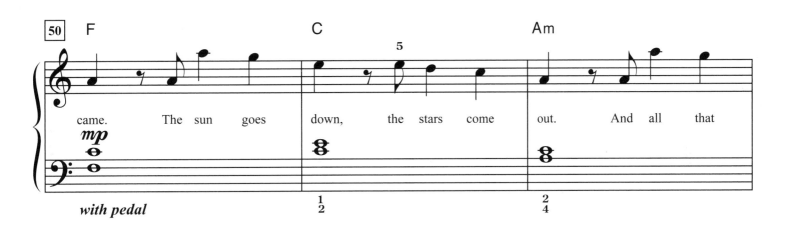

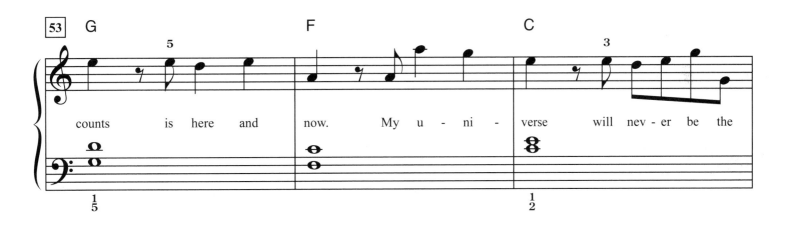

# GRENADE

Words and Music by
Claude Kelly, Peter Hernandez, Brody Brown,
Philip Lawrence, Ari Levine and Andrew Wyatt
Arranged by Carol Matz

**Moderately**

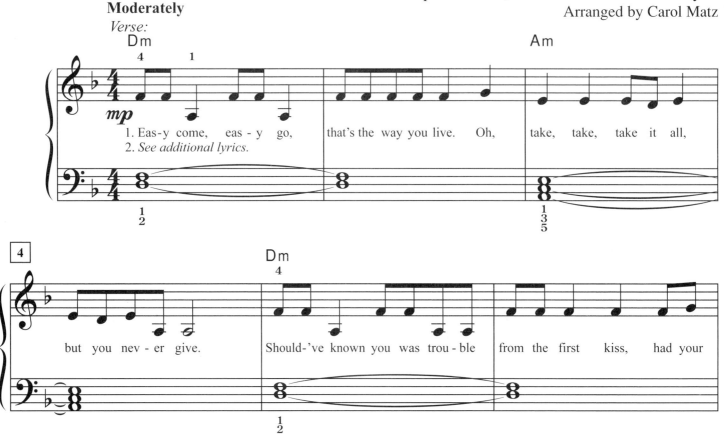

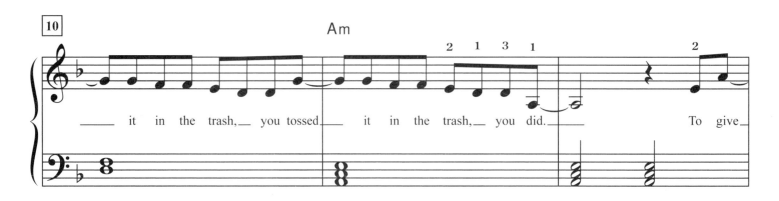

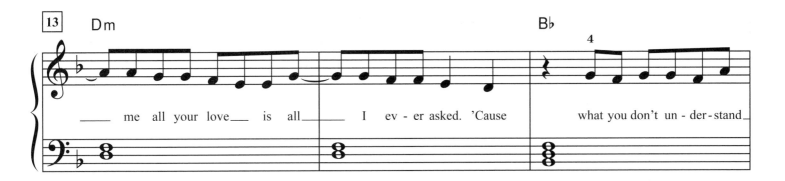

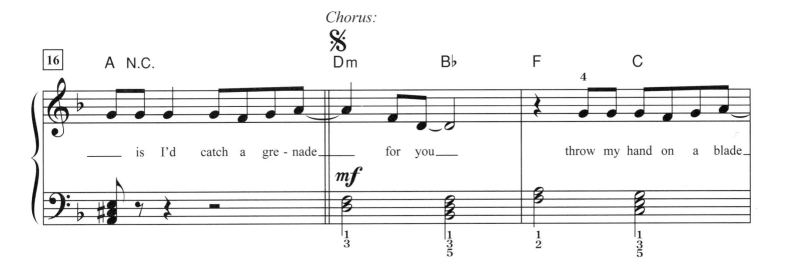

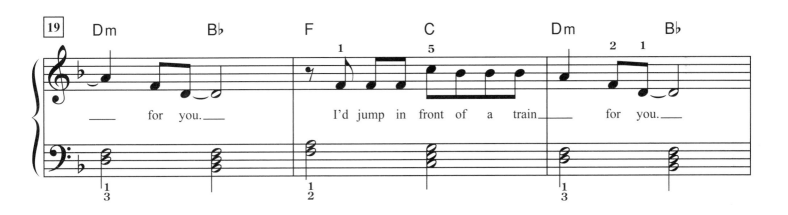

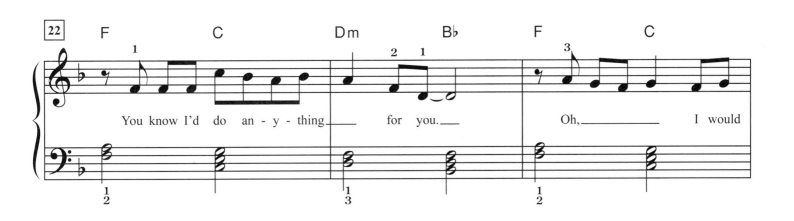

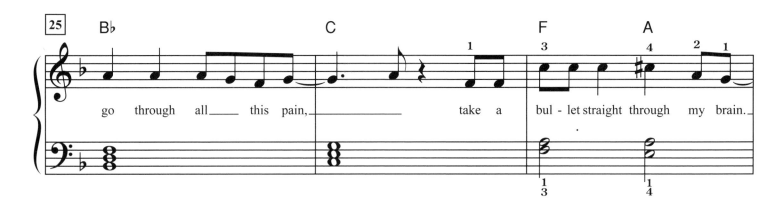

go through all\_\_\_\_\_ this pain,_____ take a bul - let straight through my brain.

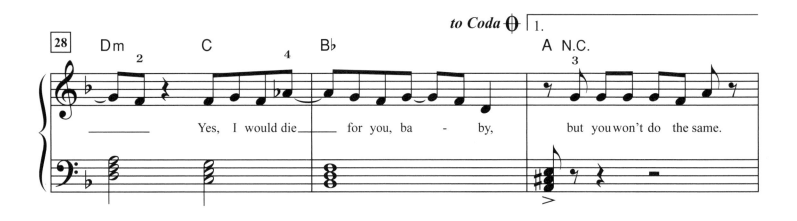

*to Coda*

Yes, I would die\_\_\_\_ for you, ba - by, but you won't do the same.

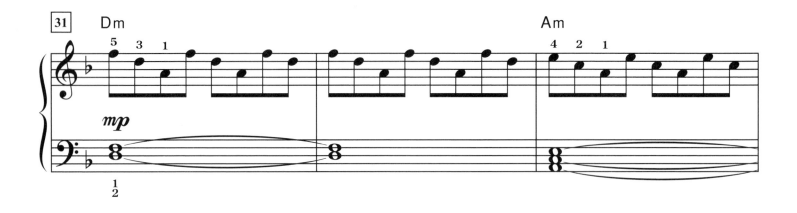

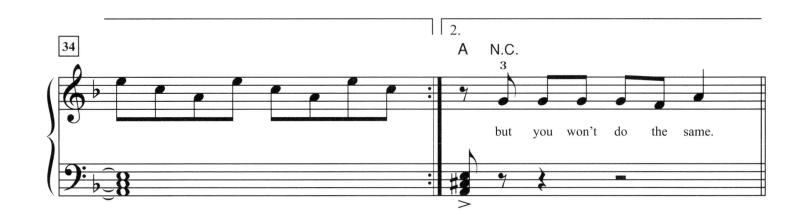

but you won't do the same.

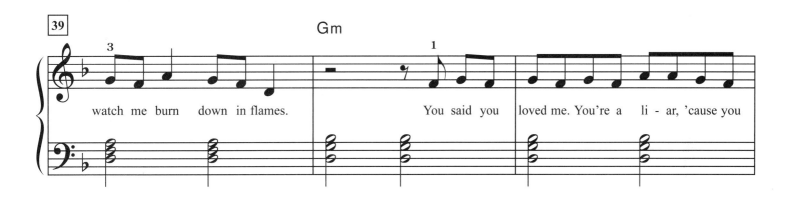

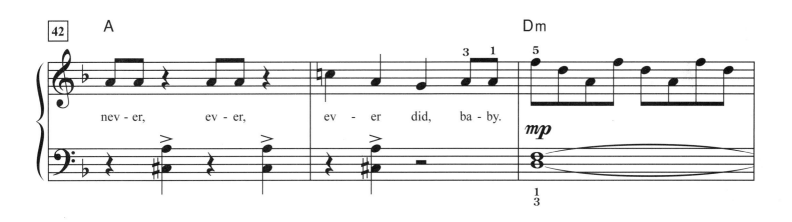

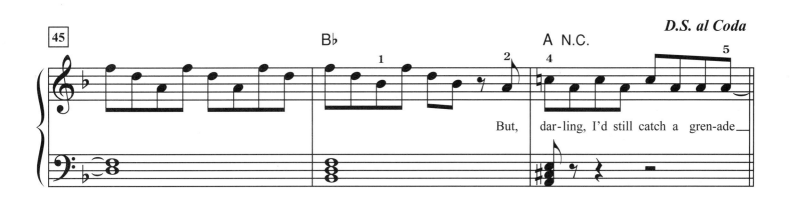

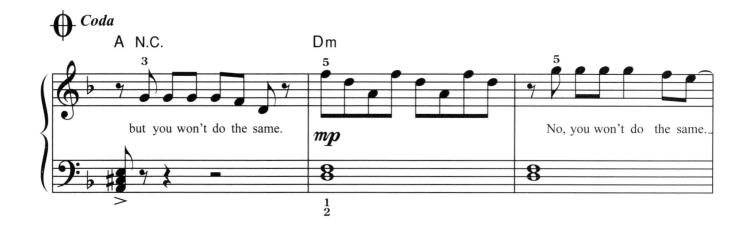

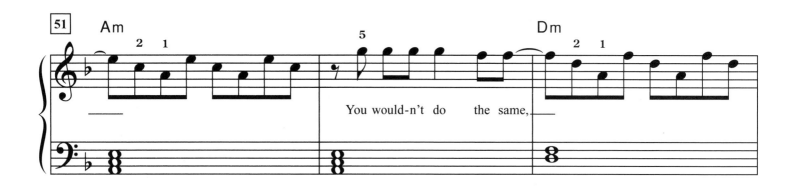

*Verse 2:*
Black, black, black and blue, beat me 'til I'm numb.
Tell the devil I said "Hey" when you get back to where you're from.
Mad woman, bad woman, that's just what you are.
Yeah, you'll smile in my face then rip the brakes out my car.
Gave you all I had and you tossed it in the trash,
You tossed it in the trash, you did.
To give me all your love is all I ever asked.
'Cause what you don't understand is I'd catch a grenade for you...
*(To Chorus:)*

# HAVEN'T MET YOU YET

Words and Music by
Michael Bublé, Alan Chang and Amy Foster
Arranged by Carol Matz

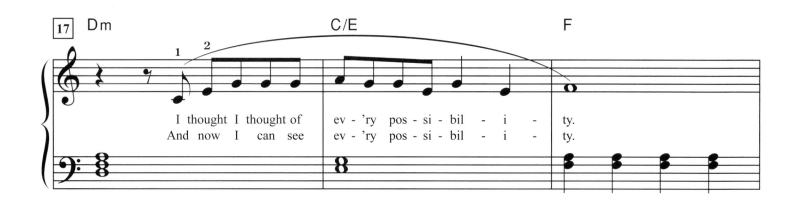

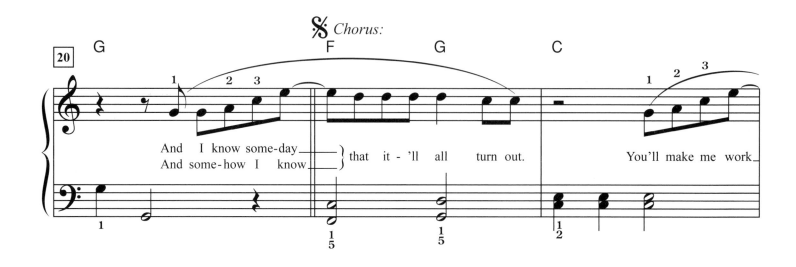

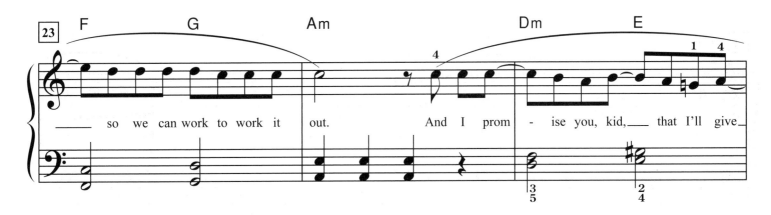

so we can work to work it out. And I prom - ise you, kid,___ that I'll give___

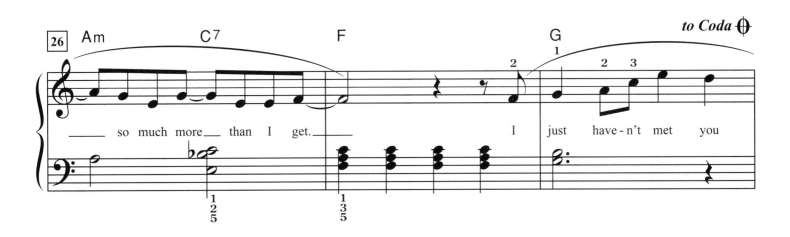

*to Coda*

___ so much more___ than I get.___ I just have - n't met you

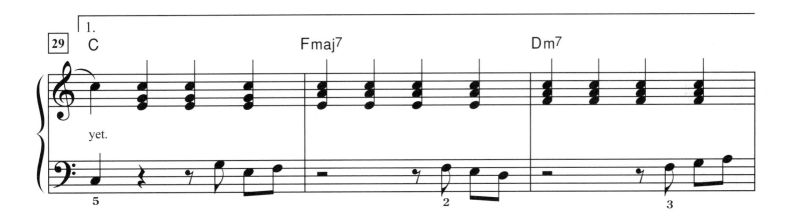

1.

yet.

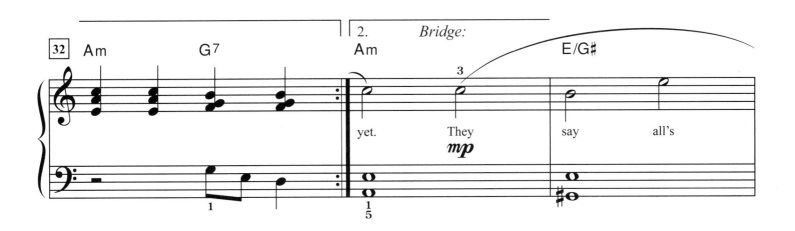

2. *Bridge:*

yet. They say all's

*mp*

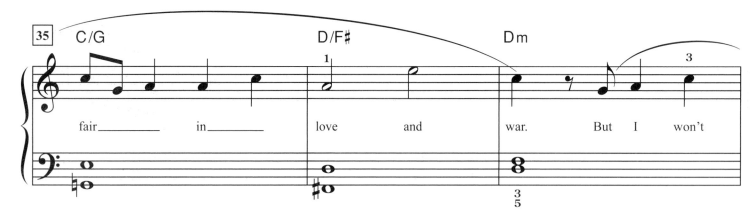

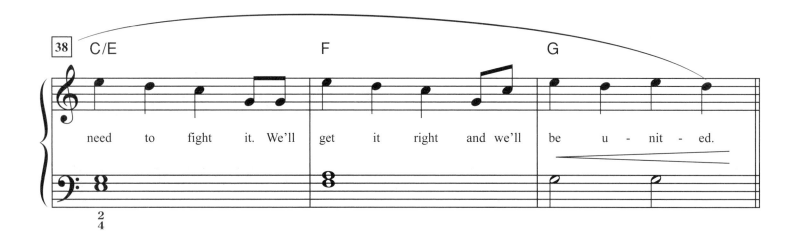

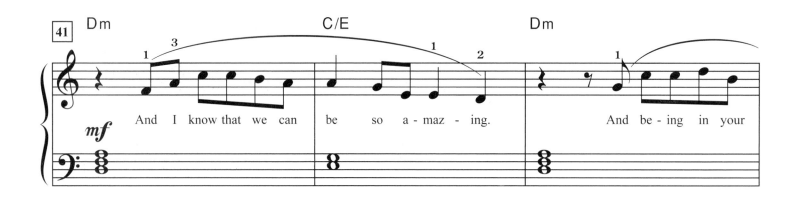

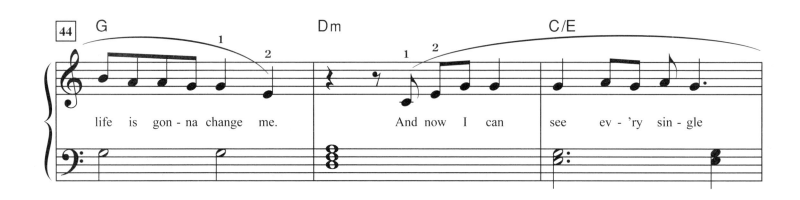

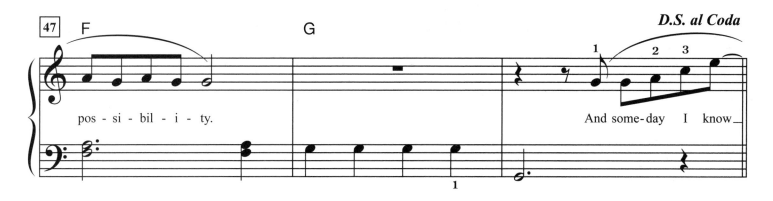

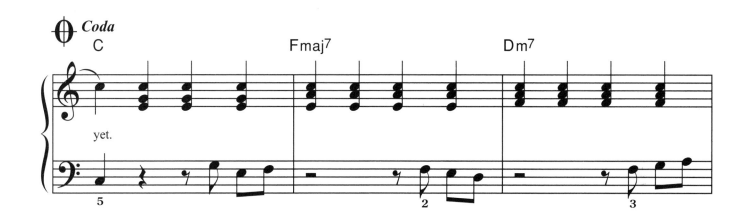

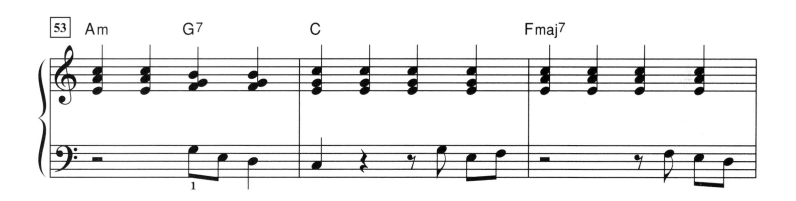

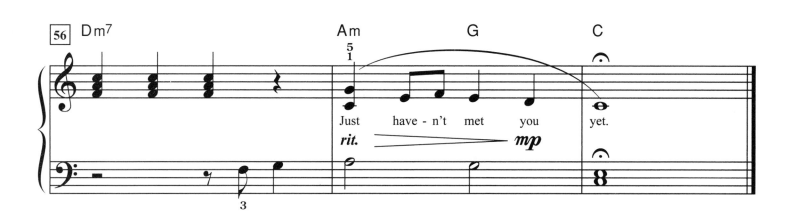

# HEY THERE DELILAH

Words and Music by Tom Higgenson
Arranged by Carol Matz

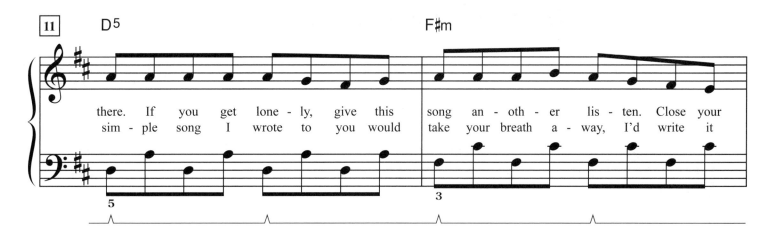

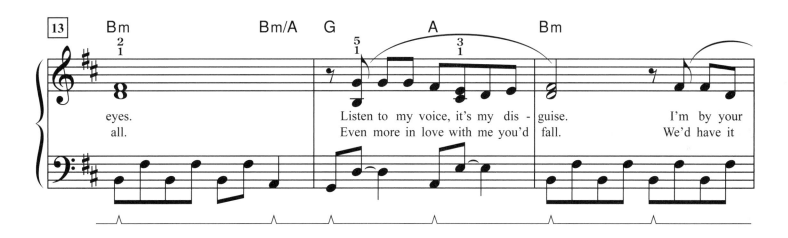

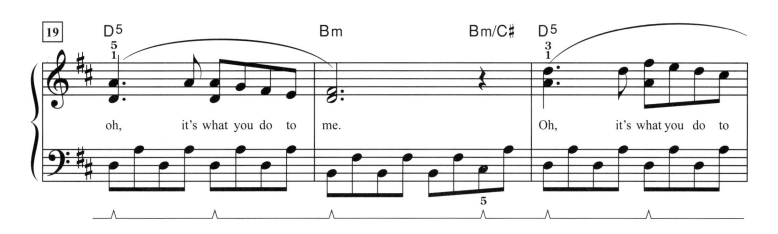

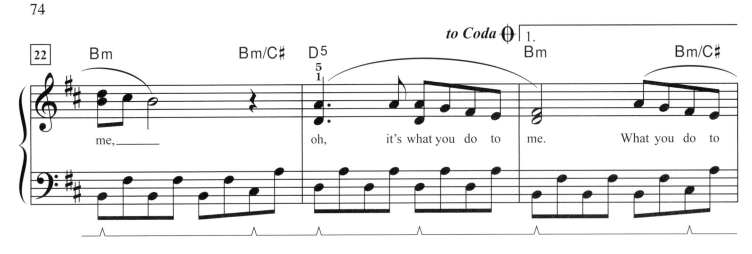

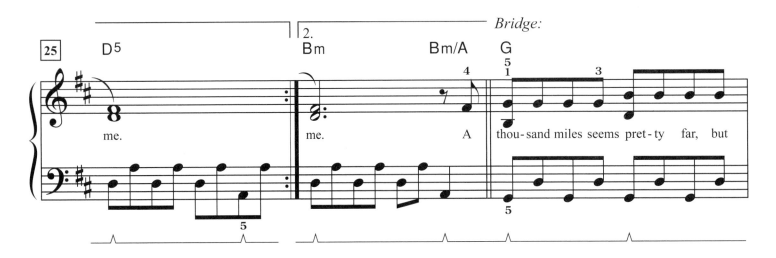

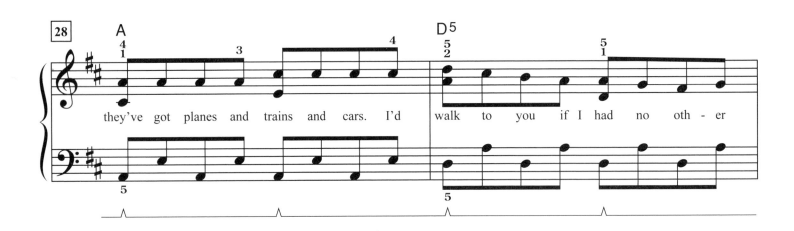

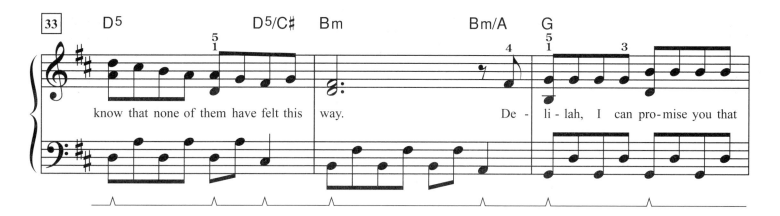

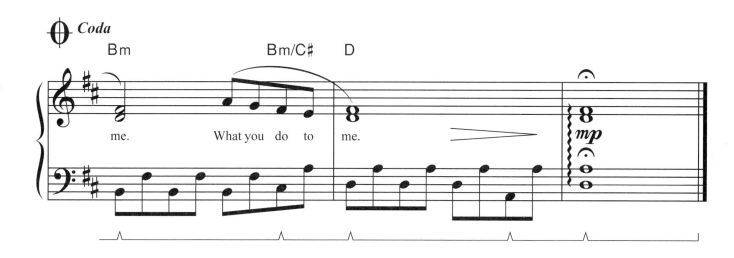

# IF I DIE YOUNG

Words and Music by Kimberly Perry
Arranged by Carol Matz

*Chorus:*

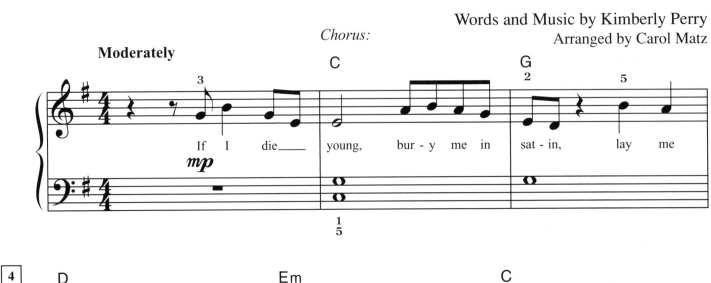

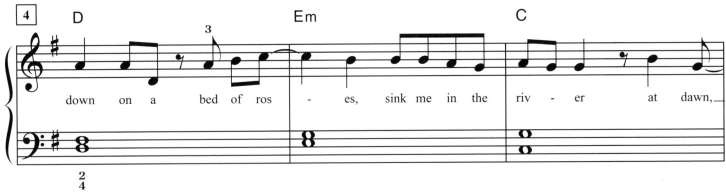

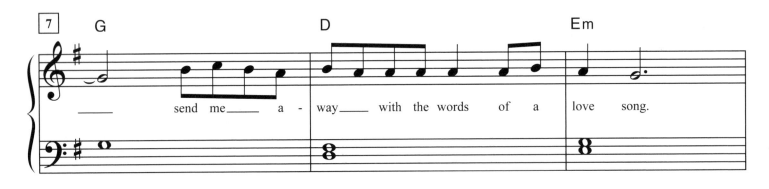

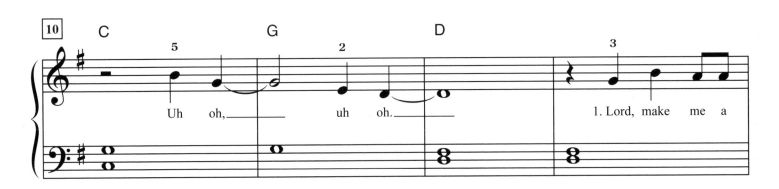

rain - bow, I'll shine down on my mother. She'll know I'm safe with
2., 3. *See additional lyrics.*

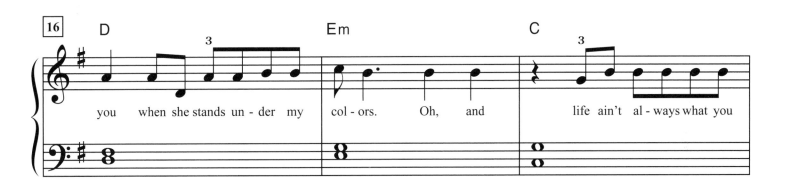

you when she stands un - der my col - ors. Oh, and life ain't al - ways what you

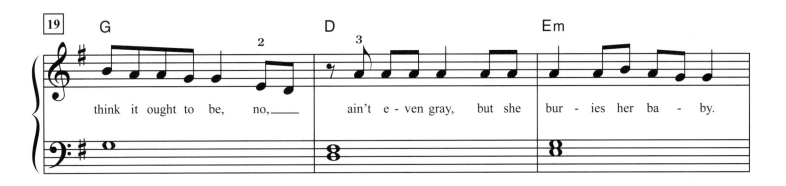

think it ought to be, no,___ ain't e - ven gray, but she bur - ies her ba - by.

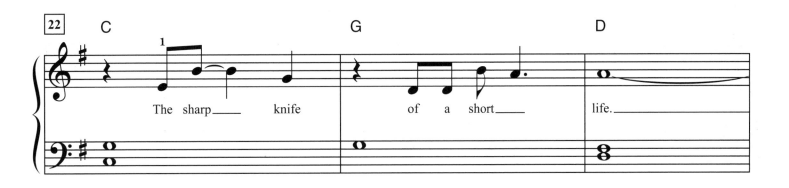

The sharp___ knife of a short___ life.___

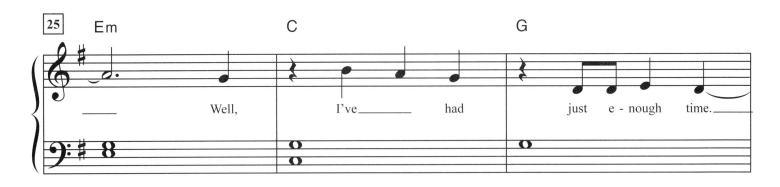

*Chorus:*

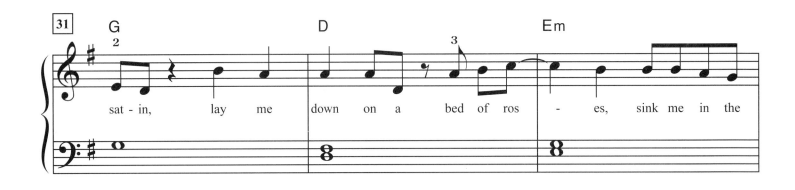

79

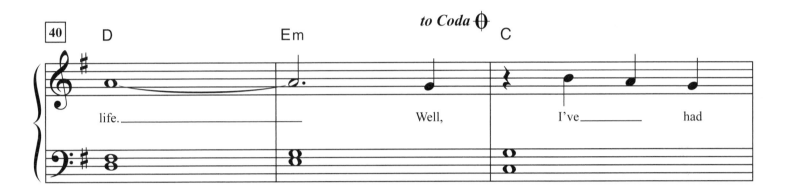

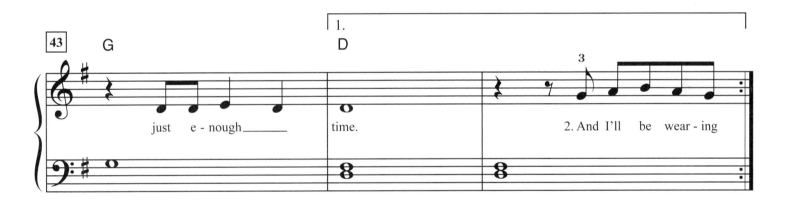

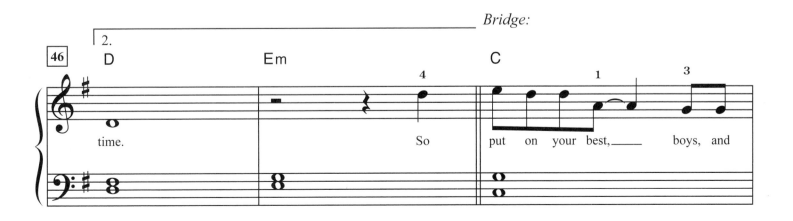

*D.S. al Coda*

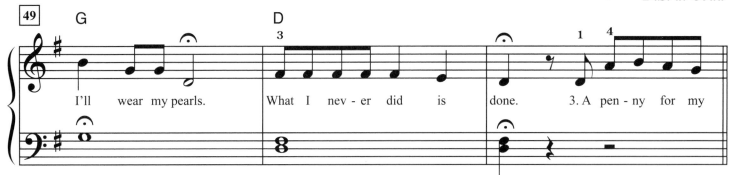

I'll wear my pearls. What I nev-er did is done. 3. A pen-ny for my

**Coda**

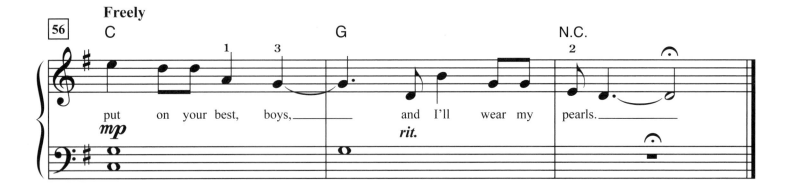

I've_____ had just e-nough time._____ So_____

*rit.*

**Freely**

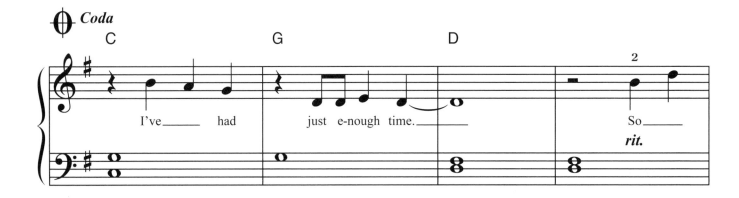

put on your best, boys,_____ and I'll wear my pearls._____

*mp* *rit.*

*Verse 2:*
And I'll be wearing white when I come into your kingdom.
I'm as green as the ring on my little cold finger.
I've never known the loving of a man,
But it sure felt nice when he was holding my hand.
There's a boy here in town, says he'll love me forever.
Who would have thought forever could be severed
By the sharp knife of a short life.
Well, I've had just enough time.

*Verse 3:*
A penny for my thoughts, oh no, I'll sell them for a dollar.
They're worth so much more after I'm a goner.
And maybe then you'll hear the words I've been singing.
Funny, when you're dead how people start list'nin'.

# JAR OF HEARTS

Words and Music by
Drew Lawrence, Christina Perri and Barrett Yeretsian
Arranged by Carol Matz

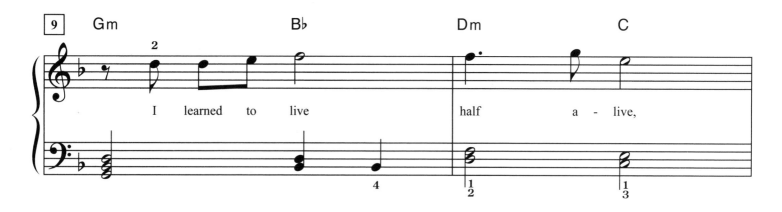

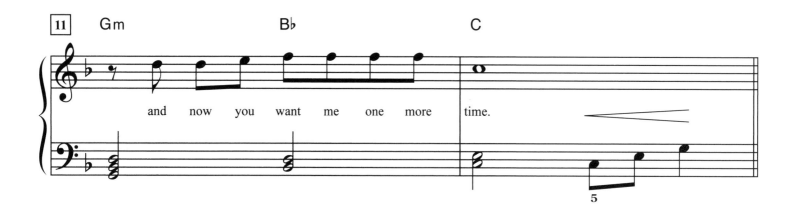

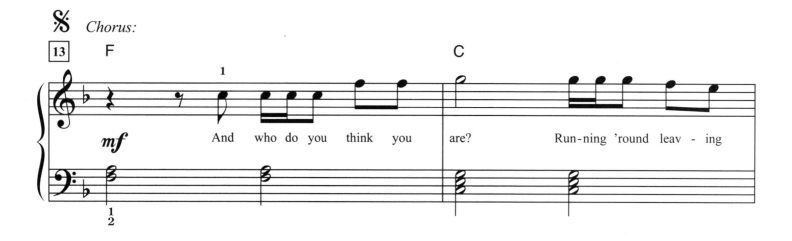

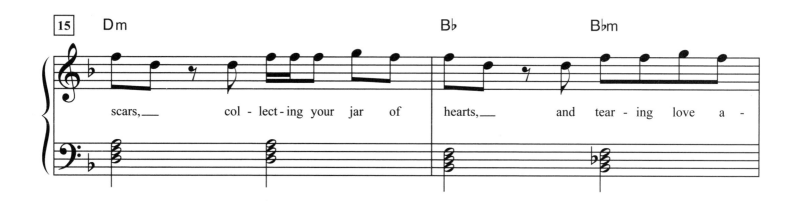

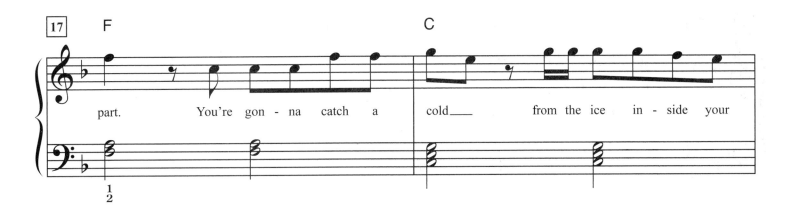

**17** F / C

part. You're gon - na catch a cold___ from the ice in - side your

*to Coda* ⊕

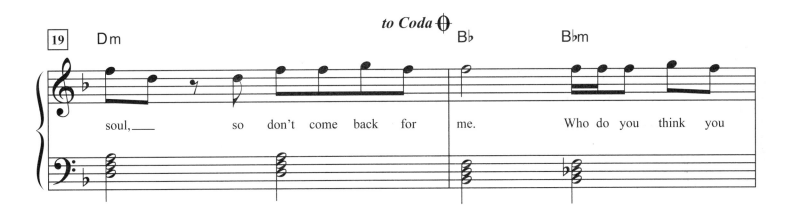

**19** Dm / B♭ / B♭m

soul,___ so don't come back for me. Who do you think you

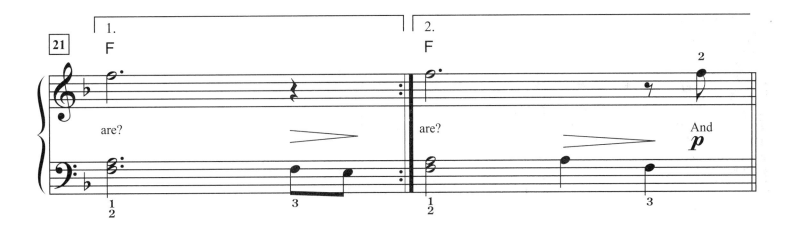

**21** 1. F / 2. F

are? / are? / And

*p*

*Bridge:*

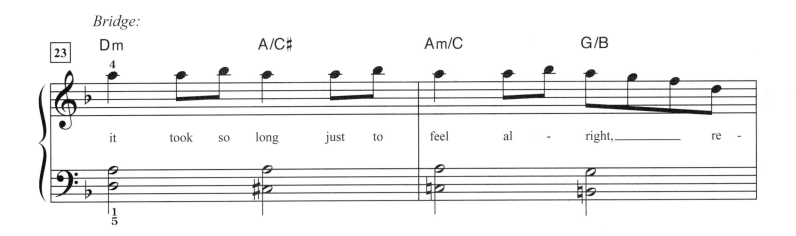

**23** Dm / A/C♯ / Am/C / G/B

it took so long just to feel al - right,_____ re -

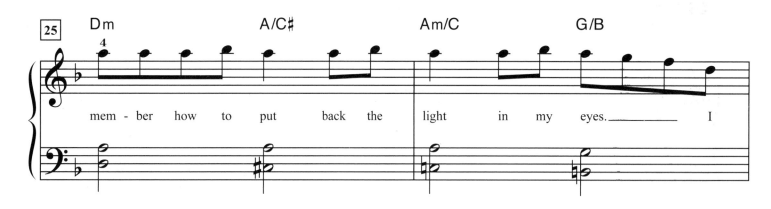

mem - ber how to put back the light in my eyes._____ I

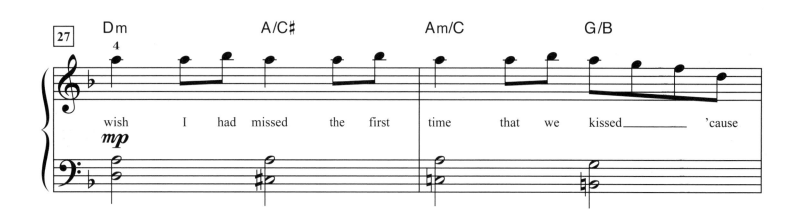

wish I had missed the first time that we kissed_____ 'cause

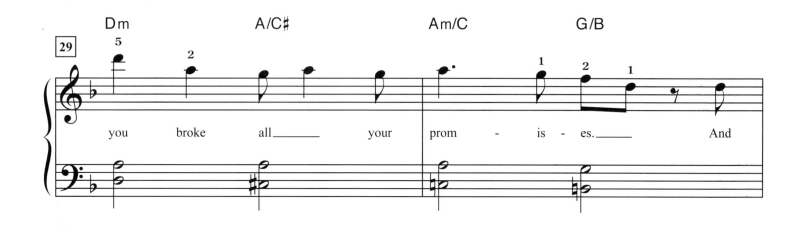

you broke all_____ your prom - is - es._____ And

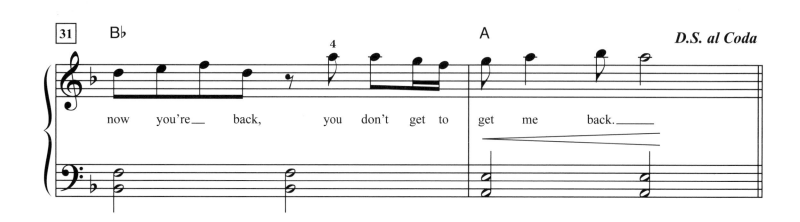

now you're__ back, you don't get to get me back._____

Verse 2:
I heard you're asking all around
If I am anywhere to be found.
But I have grown too strong
To ever fall back in your arms.
And I learned to live half alive,
And now you want me one more time.
*(To Chorus:)*

# JUST THE WAY YOU ARE (AMAZING)

Words and Music by
Khalil Walton, Peter Hernandez,
Philip Lawrence, Ari Levine and Khari Cain
Arranged by Carol Matz

**Moderately**

*Verse:*

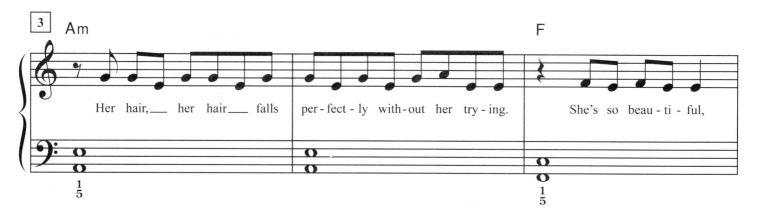

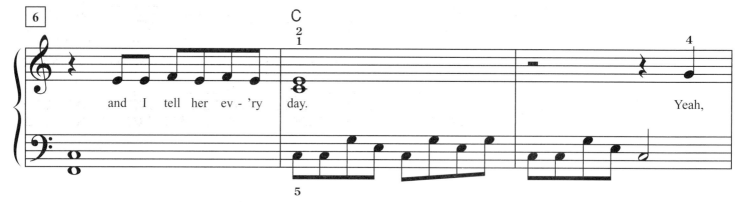

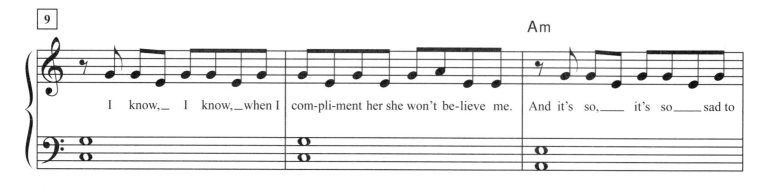

think that she don't see what I see. But ev-'ry time she asks me, "Do I look o-kay?" I

*Chorus:*

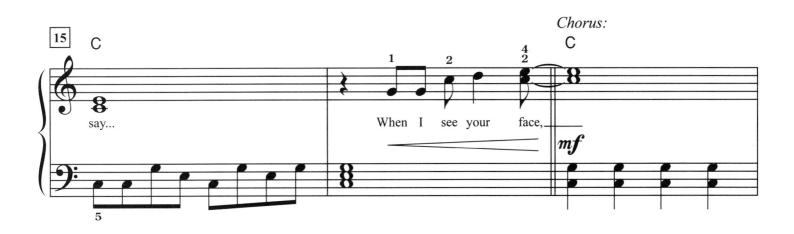

say... When I see your face,

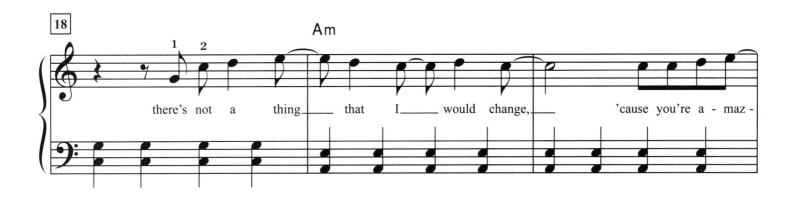

there's not a thing___ that I___ would change,___ 'cause you're a - maz-

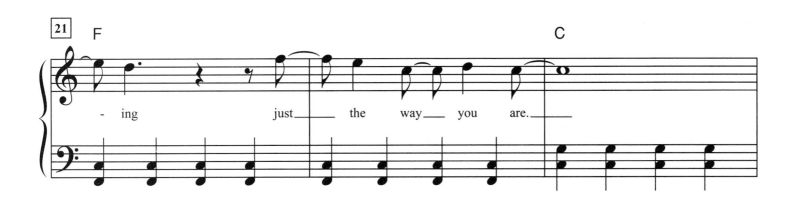

- ing just___ the way___ you are.

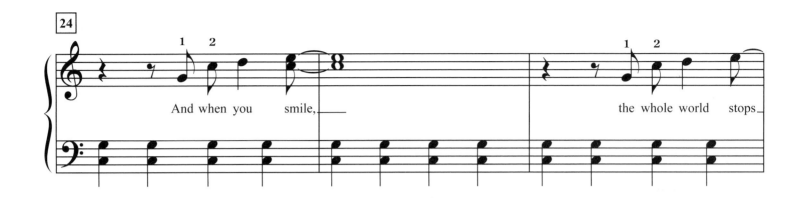

And when you smile,\_\_\_\_ the whole world stops\_

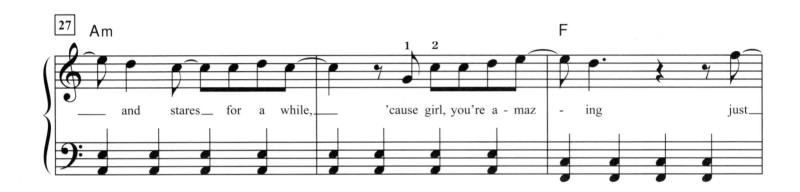

\_\_ and stares\_ for a while,\_ 'cause girl, you're a - maz - ing just\_

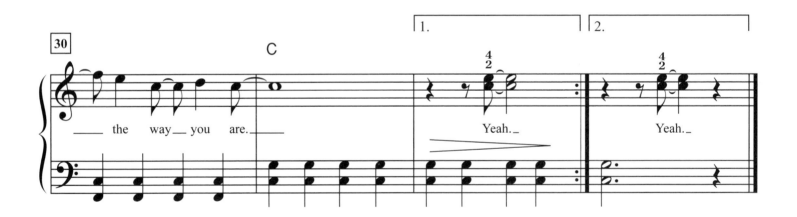

\_\_ the way\_ you are.\_\_\_ Yeah.\_ Yeah.\_

*Verse 2:*
Her lips, her lips, I could kiss them all day if she'd let me.
Her laugh, her laugh she hates, but I think it's so sexy.
She's so beautiful and I tell her every day.
Oh, you know, you know, you know I'd never ask you to change.
If perfect's what you're searching for, then just stay the same.
So don't even bother asking if you look okay. You know I'll say...
*(To Chorus:)*

# LET ME BE YOUR STAR

Lyrics by Scott Wittman and Marc Shaiman
Music by Marc Shaiman
Arranged by Carol Matz

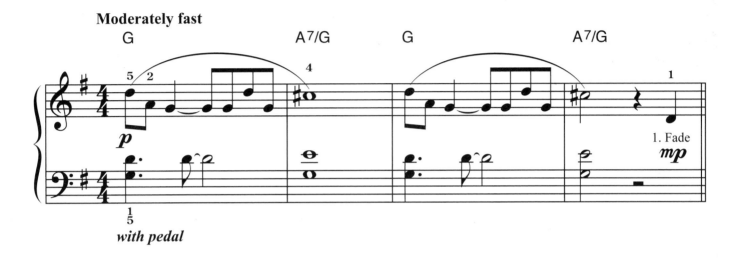

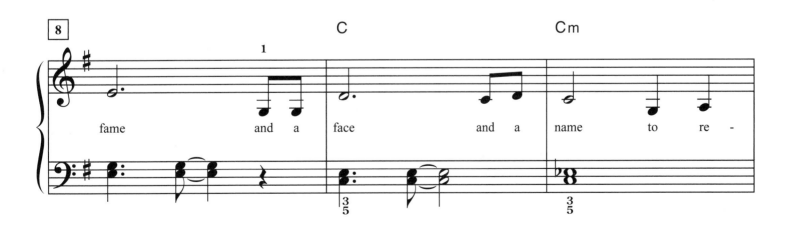

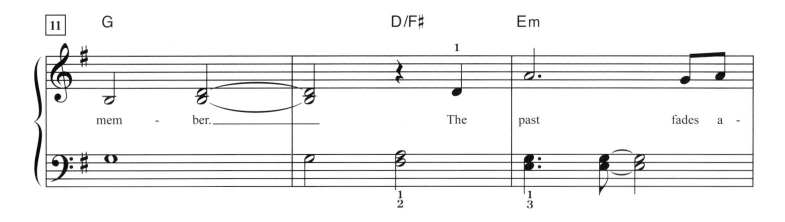

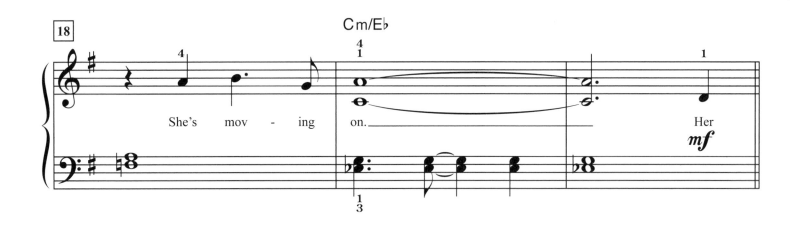

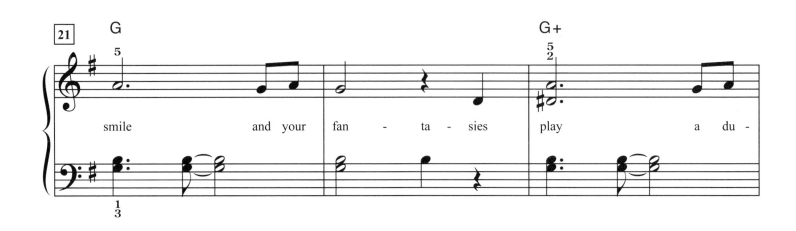

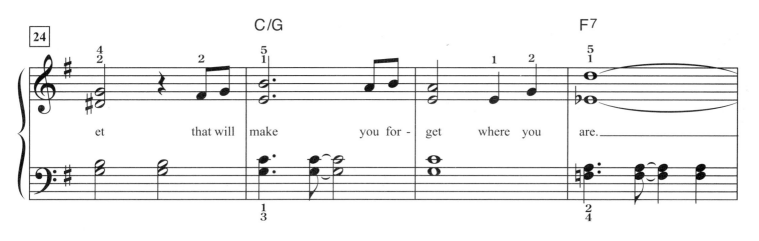

et ... that will make ... you for - get ... where you ... are.\_\_\_

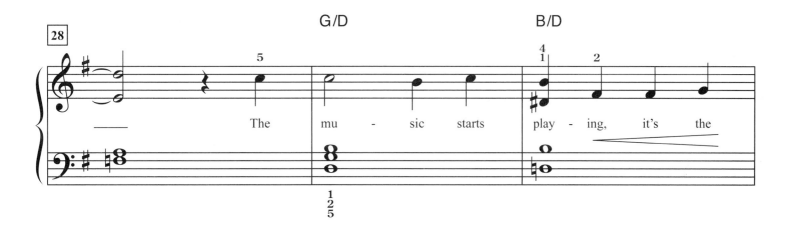

\_\_\_ The ... mu - sic ... starts ... play - ing, ... it's ... the

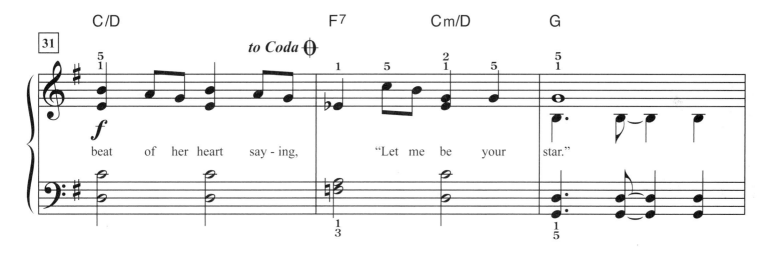

beat ... of ... her ... heart ... say - ing, ... "Let ... me ... be ... your ... star."

2. Flash

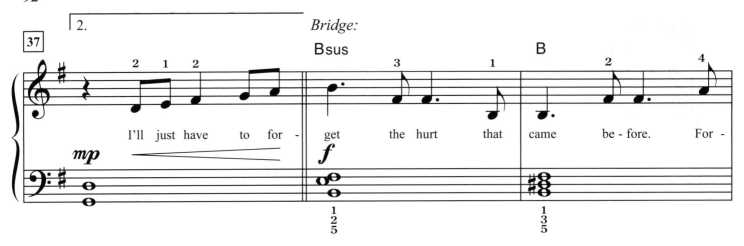

2.

*Bridge:*

I'll just have to for - get the hurt that came be - fore. For -

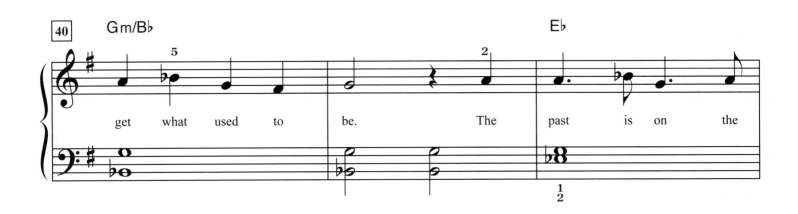

get what used to be. The past is on the

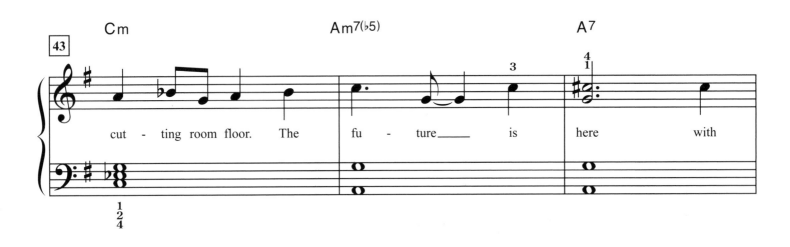

cut - ting room floor. The fu - ture___ is here with

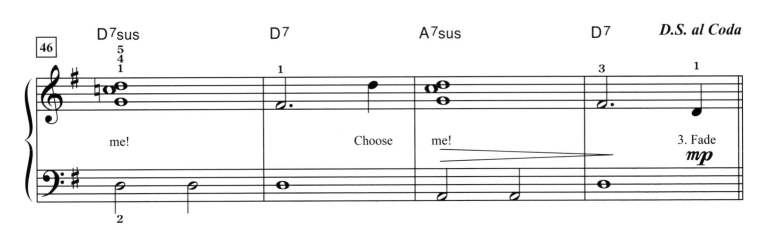

*D.S. al Coda*

me! Choose me! 3. Fade

**Coda**

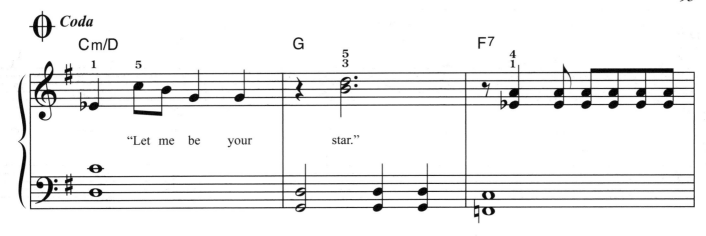

"Let me be your star."

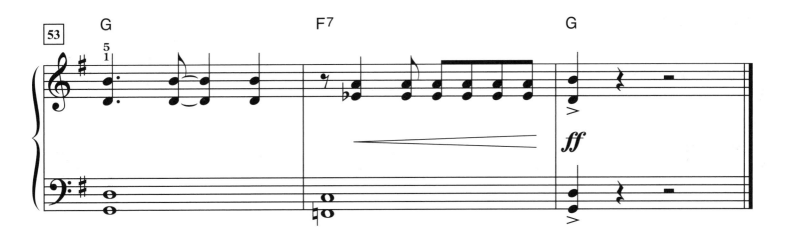

*Verse 2:*

Flash back to a girl with a song in her heart
As she's waiting to start the adventure.
The fire and drive that make dreams come alive,
They fill her soul. She's in control.
The drama, the laughter, the tears just like pearls,
Well, they're all in this girl's repertoire.
It's all for the taking and it's magic we'll be making,
Let me be your star.

*Verse 3:*

Fade up on a star with it all in her sights,
All the love and the lights that surround her.
Someday she'll think twice of the dues and the price
She'll have to pay, but not today!
She'll do all she can for the love of one man
And for millions who love from afar.
I'm what you've been needing, it's all here and her heart's pleading,
Let me be your star.

# LOVE YOU LIKE A LOVE SONG

Words and Music by
Antonina Armato, Adam Schmalholz and Tim James
Arranged by Carol Matz

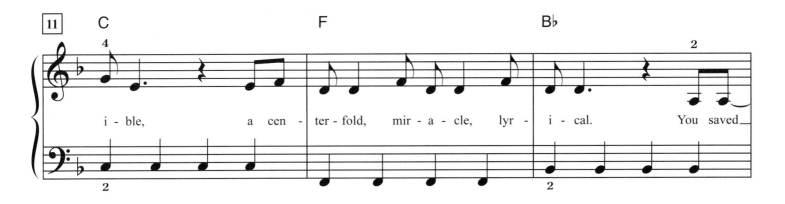

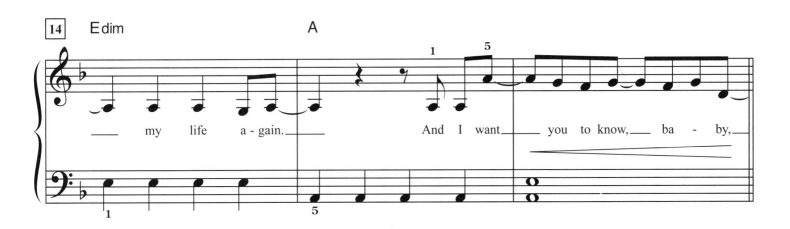

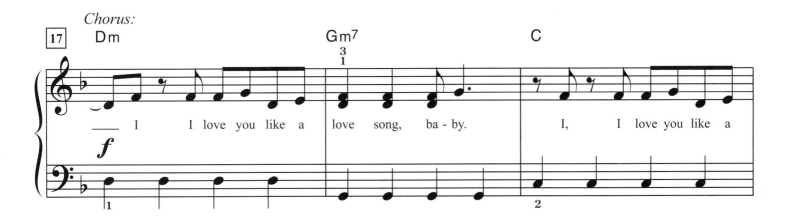

96

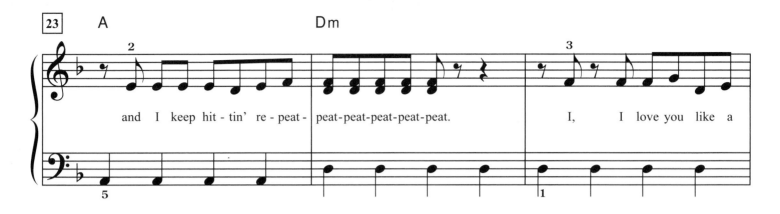

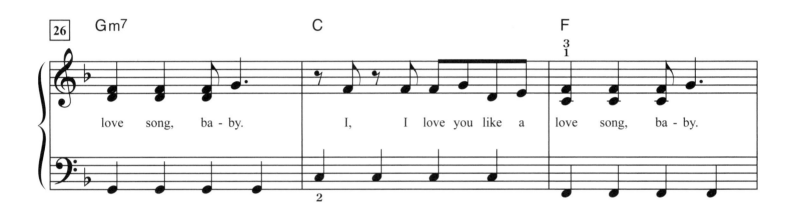

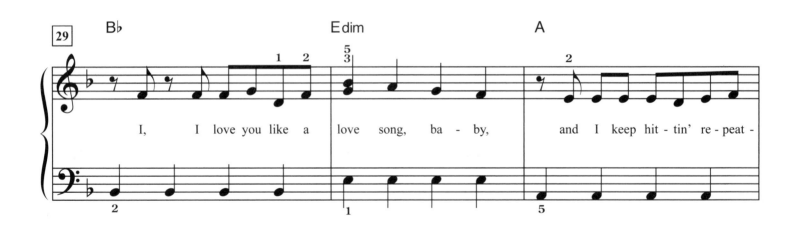

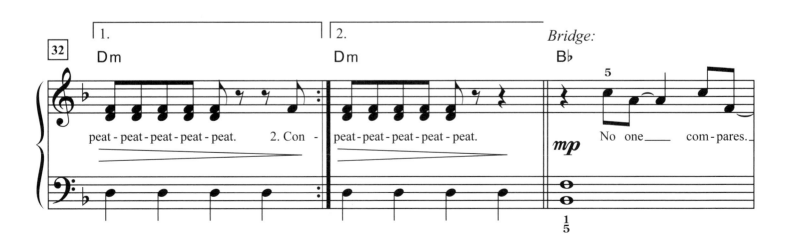

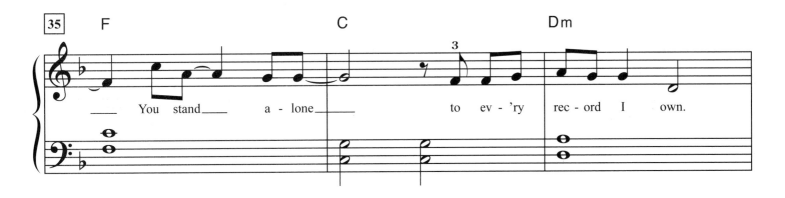

*Chorus:*

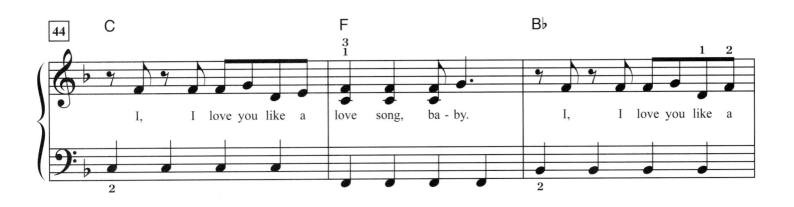

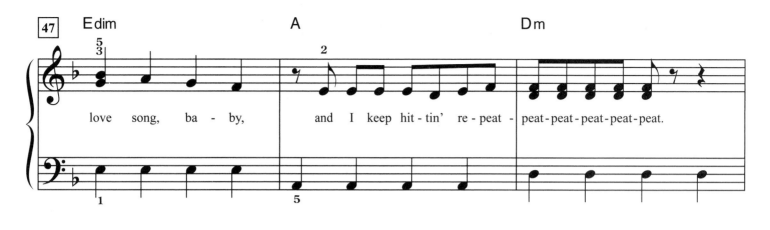

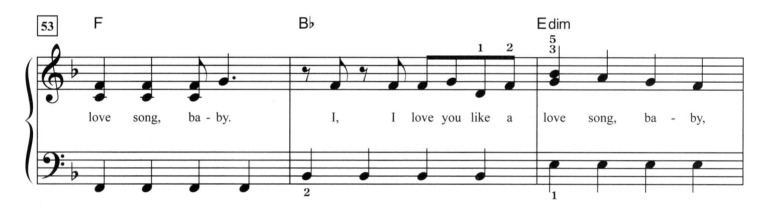

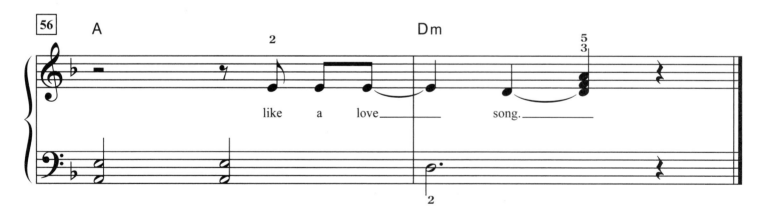

*Verse 2:*
Constantly, boy, you played through my mind like a symphony.
There's no way to describe what you do to me,
You just do to me what you do.
And it feels like I've been rescued, I've been set free.
I am hypnotized by your destiny.
You are magical, lyrical, beautiful.
You are. And I want you to know, baby,
*(To Chorus:)*

# NOT LIKE THE MOVIES

Words and Music by
Katy Perry and Greg Wells
Arranged by Carol Matz

100

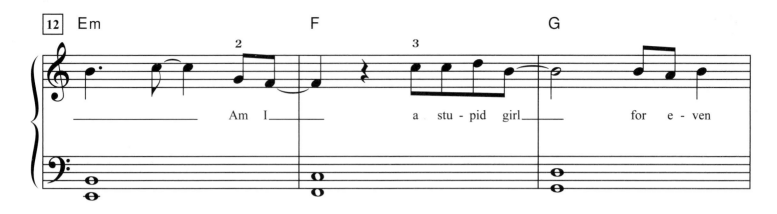

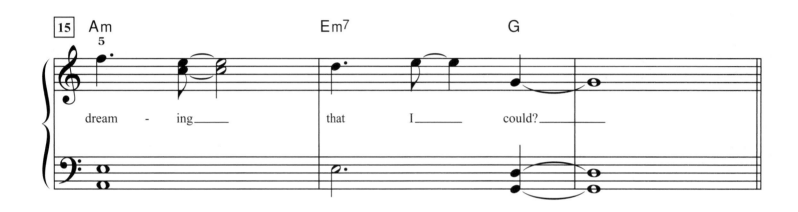

Chorus:

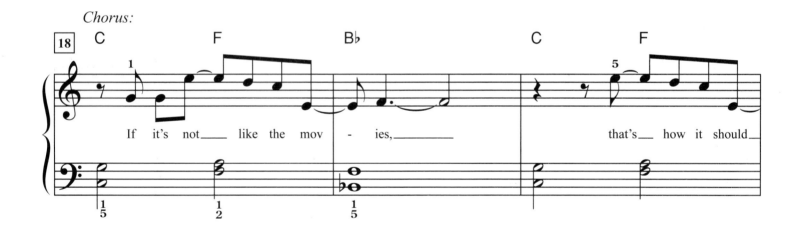

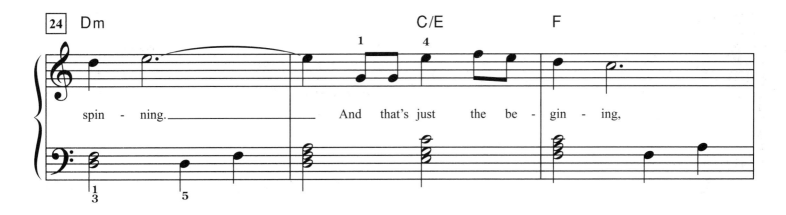

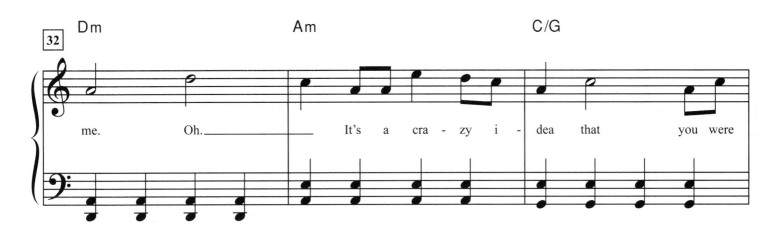

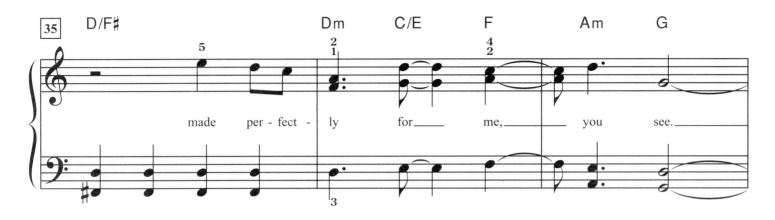

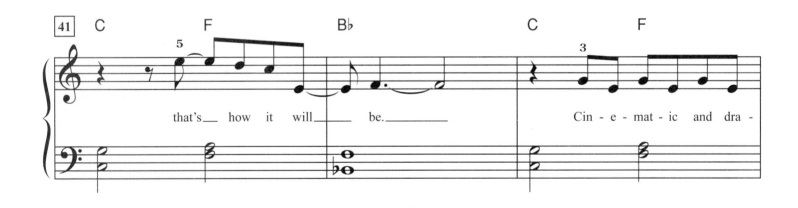

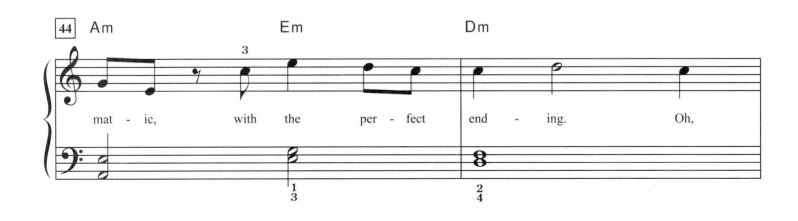

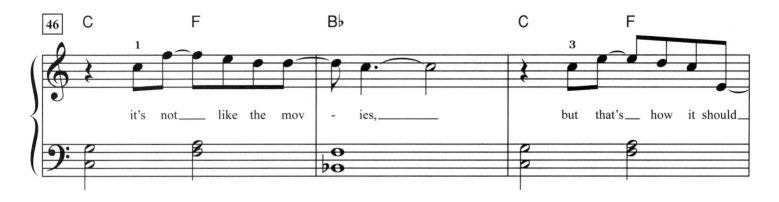

it's not___ like the mov - ies,_____ but that's___ how it should___

___ be.___ When he's the one, you'll come un - done, and your world will stop

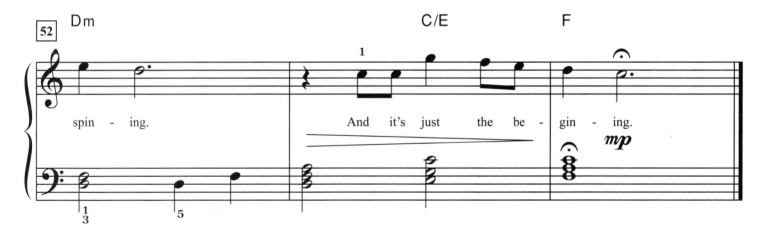

spin - ing. And it's just the be - gin - ing.

*Verse 2:*
Snow White said when I was young,
"One day my prince will come."
So I wait for that date.
They say it's hard to meet your match,
Gotta find my better half,
So we make perfect shapes.
If stars don't align, if it doesn't stop time,
If you can't see the sign, wait for it.
One hundred percent, worth every penny spent,
He'll be the one that finishes your sentences.
*(To Chorus:)*

# NEED YOU NOW

Words and Music by Dave Haywood,
Charles Kelley, Hillary Scott and Josh Kear
Arranged by Carol Matz

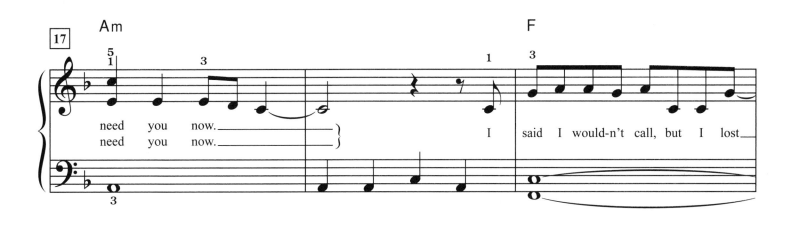

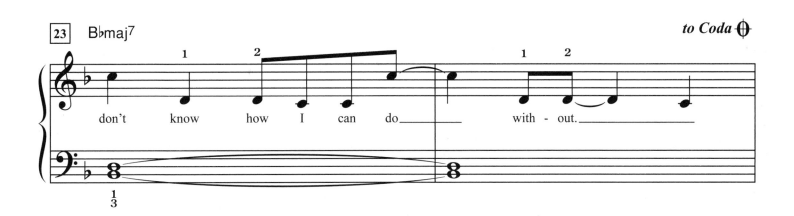

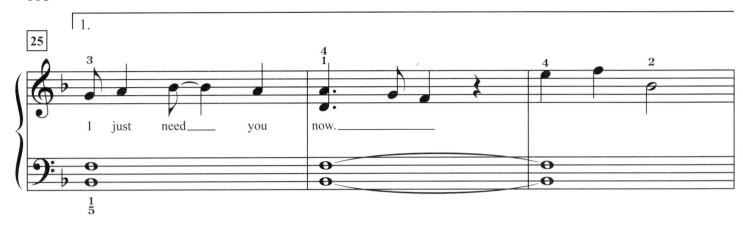

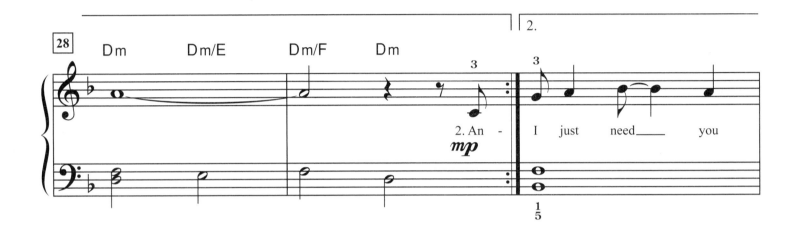

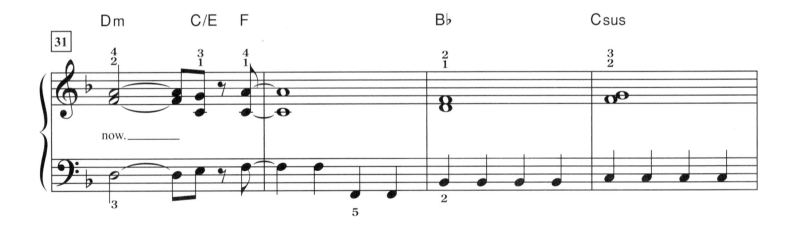

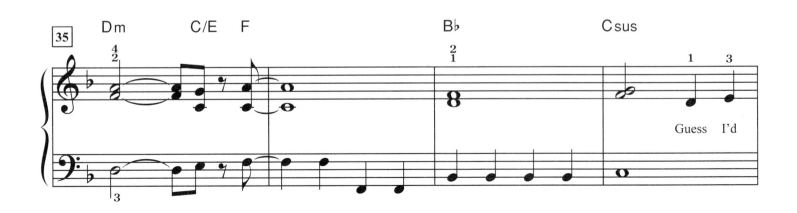

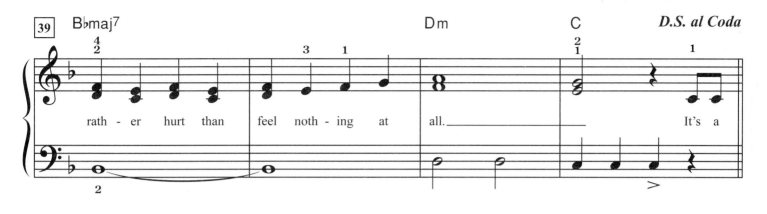

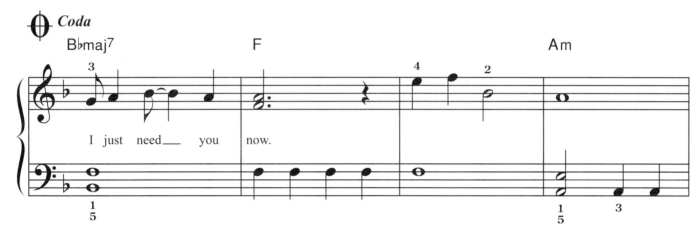

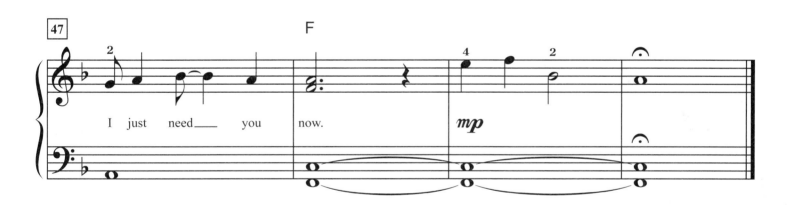

*Verse 2:*
Another shot of whiskey, can't stop looking at the door,
Wishing you'd come sweeping in the way you did before.
And I wonder if I ever cross your mind.
For me it happens all the time.

# NOT OVER YOU

Words and Music by
Gavin Degraw and Ryan Tedder
Arranged by Carol Matz

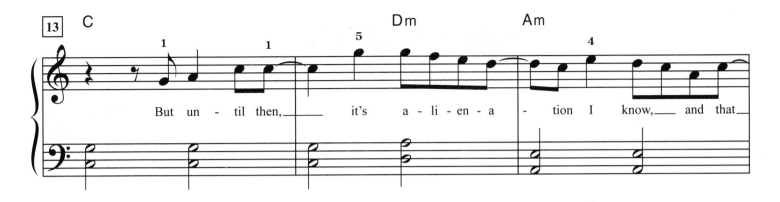

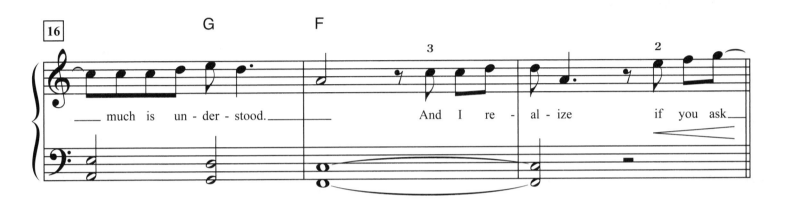

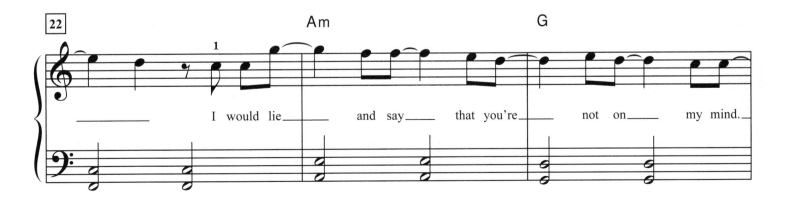

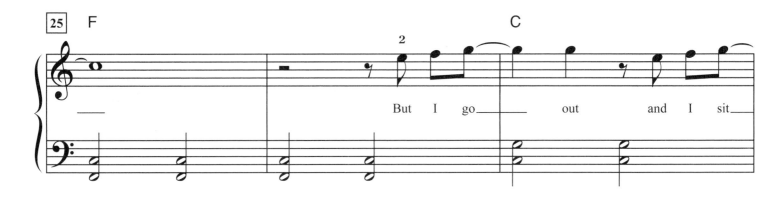

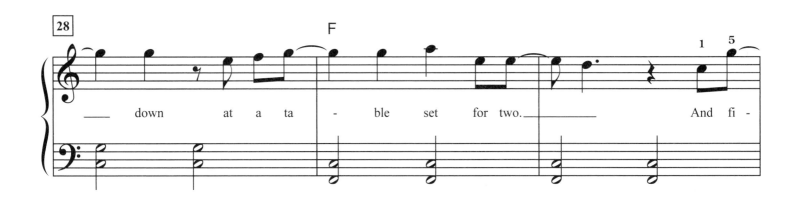

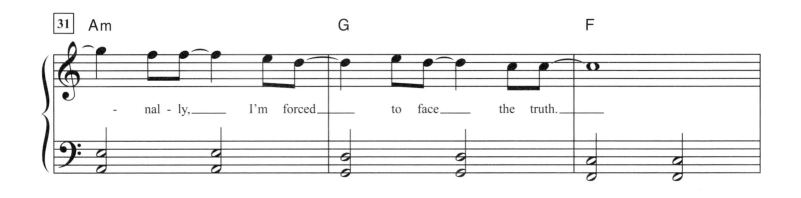

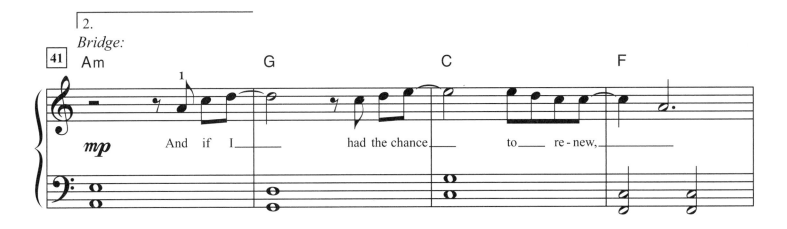

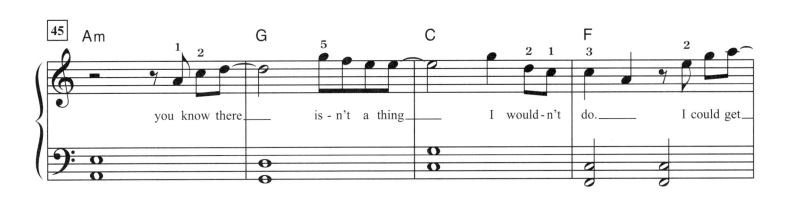

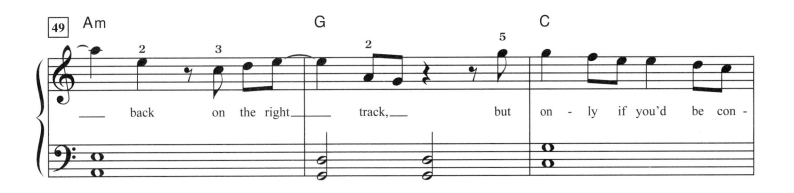

vinced._____    So un-til then,_____    if you ask__

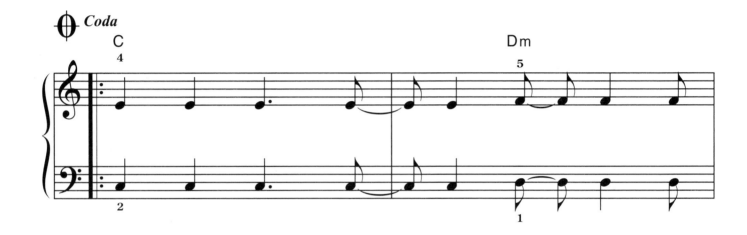

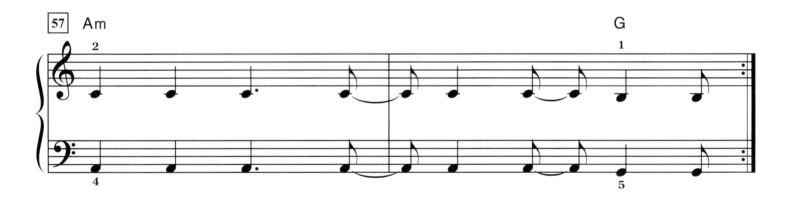

*Verse 2:*
Damn, damn, girl, you do it well.
And I thought you were innocent.
Took this heart and put it through hell,
But still, you're magnificent.
I, I'm a boomerang.
Doesn't matter how you throw me,
Turn around, and I'm back in the game,
Even better than the old me.
But I'm not even close without you.
*(To Chorus:)*

# PAYPHONE

Words and Music by
Wiz Khalifa, Adam Levine, Benjamin Levin,
Ammar Malik, Johan Schuster and Daniel Omelio
Arranged by Carol Matz

114

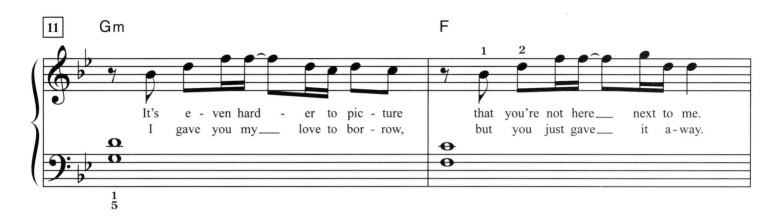

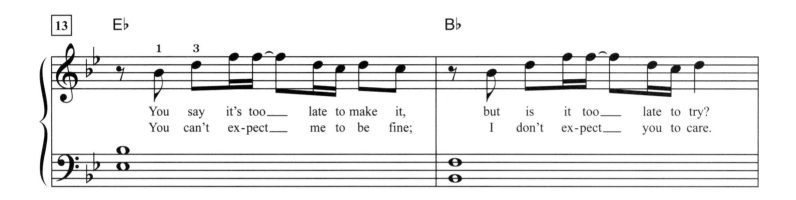

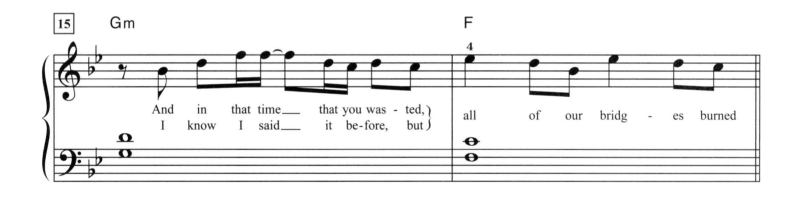

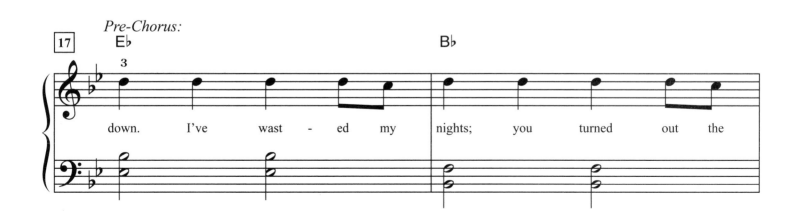

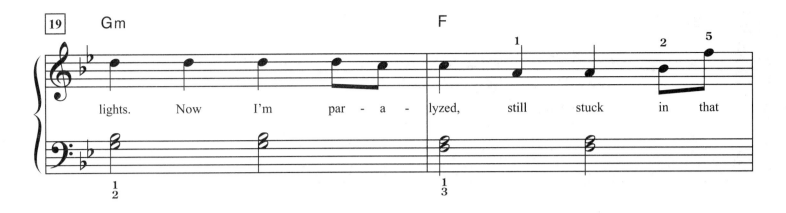

**19** | **Gm** ... **F**

lights. Now I'm par - a - lyzed, still stuck in that

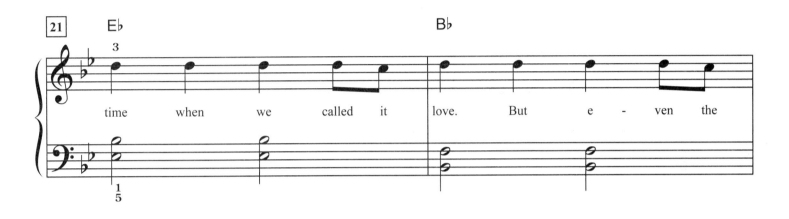

**21** | **E♭** ... **B♭**

time when we called it love. But e - ven the

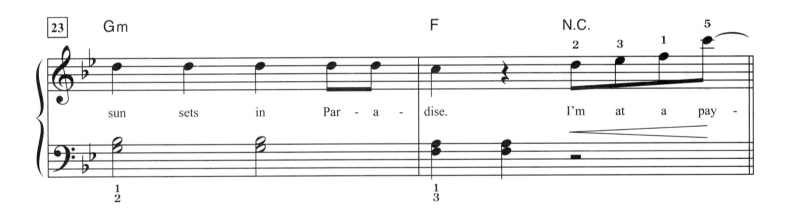

**23** | **Gm** ... **F** ... **N.C.**

sun sets in Par - a - dise. I'm at a pay -

*Chorus:*

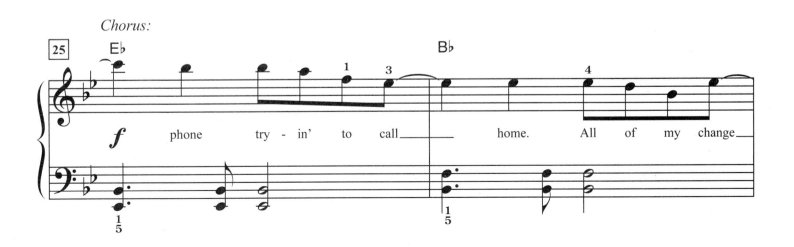

**25** | **E♭** ... **B♭**

*f* phone try - in' to call___ home. All of my change___

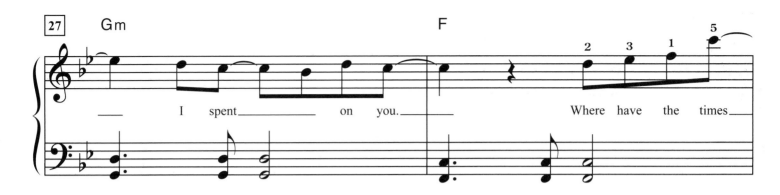

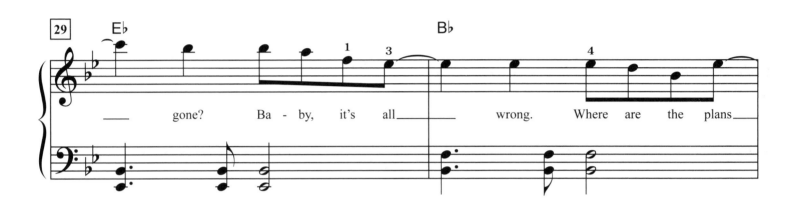

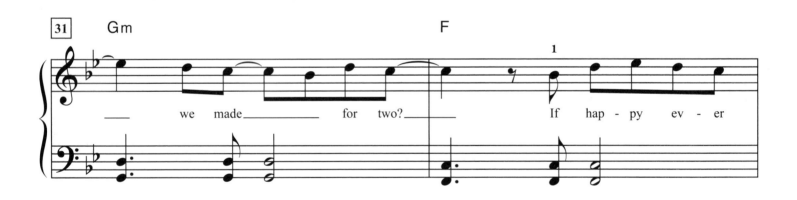

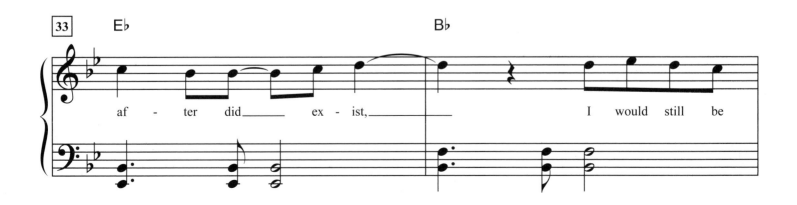

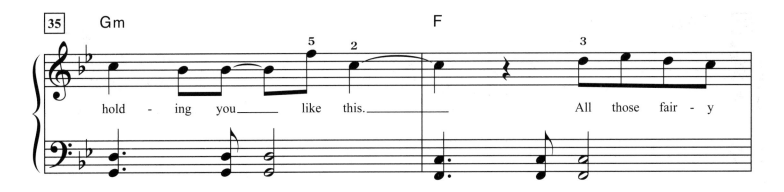

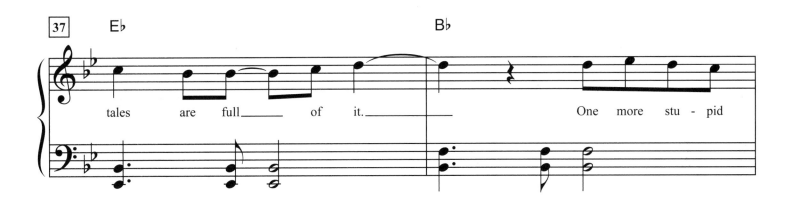

# THE ONLY EXCEPTION

Words and Music by
Hayley Williams and Josh Farro
Arranged by Carol Matz

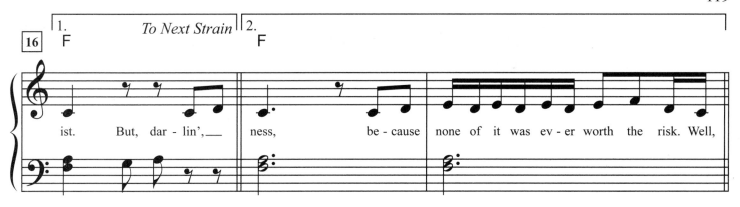

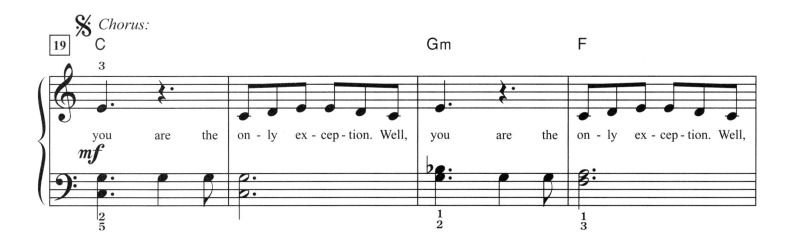

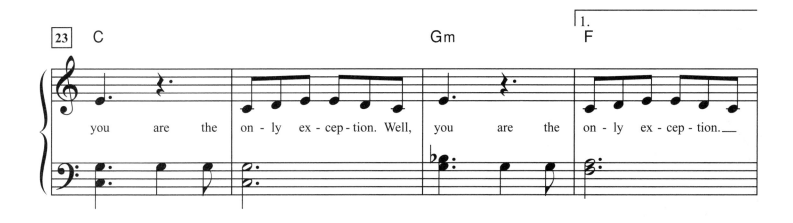

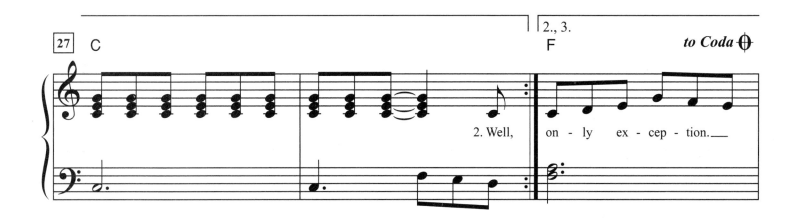

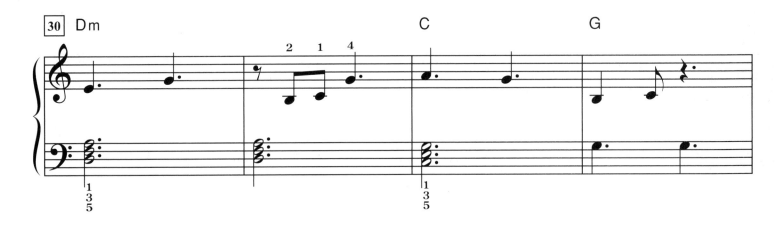

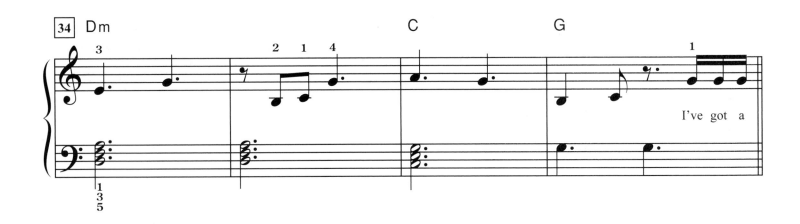

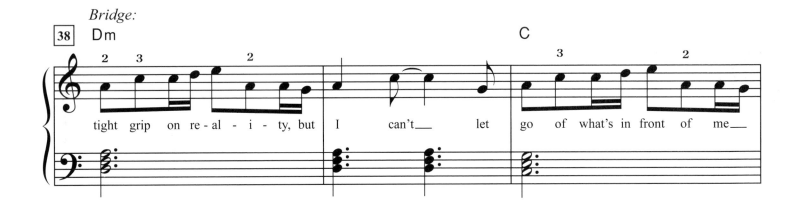

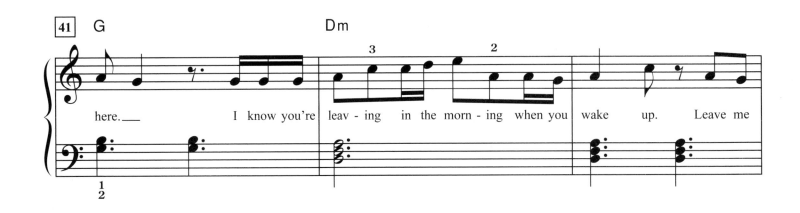

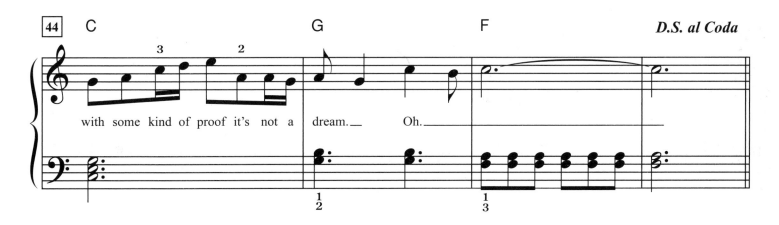

with some kind of proof it's not a dream.___ Oh.___

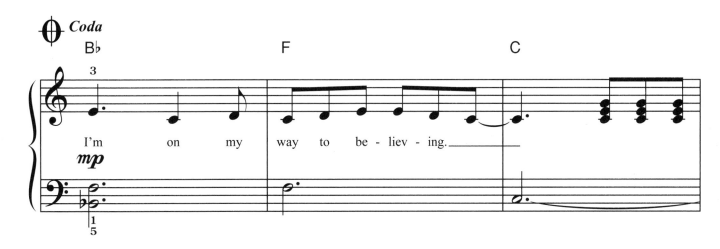

I'm on my way to be - liev - ing.___

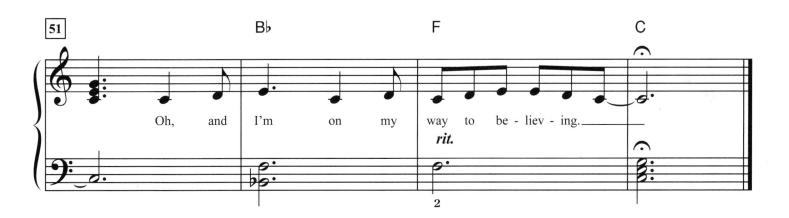

Oh, and I'm on my way to be - liev - ing.___

*Verse 2:*
Well, maybe I know somewhere
Deep in my soul
That love never lasts.
And we've got to find other ways
To make it alone,
Or keep a straight face.
And I've always lived like this,
Keeping a comfortable distance.
And up until now I had sworn to myself
That I'm content with loneliness,
Because none of it was ever worth the risk.
*(To Chorus:)*

# SECONDHAND WHITE BABY GRAND

## (from *SMASH*)

Lyrics by Scott Wittman and Marc Shaiman
Music by Marc Shaiman
Arranged by Carol Matz

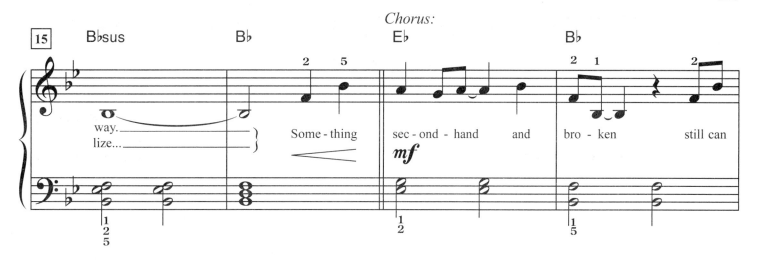

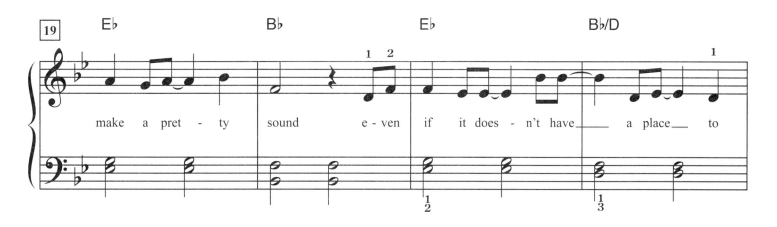

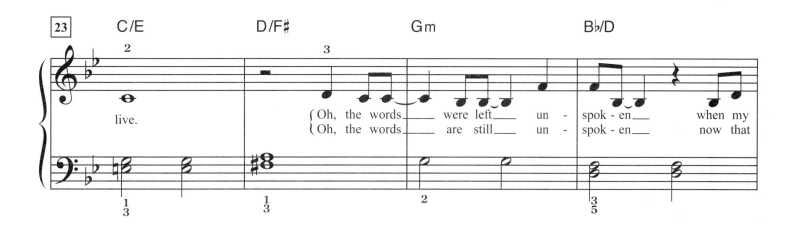

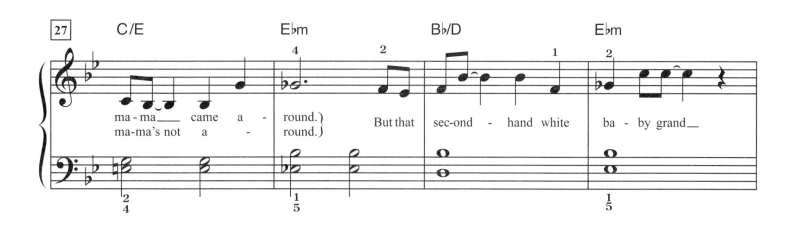

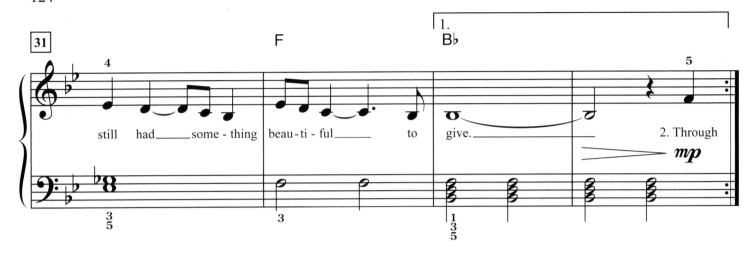

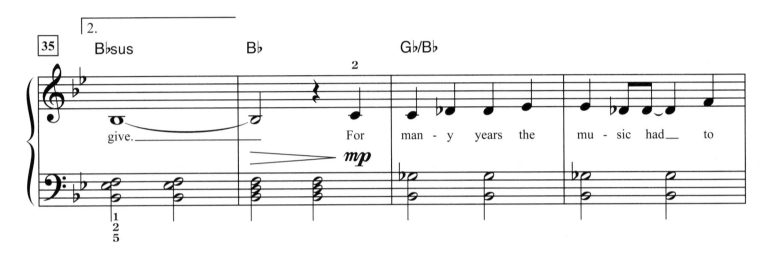

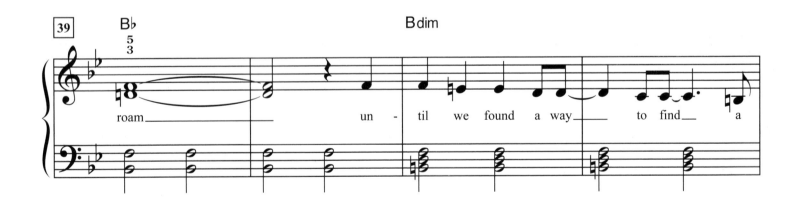

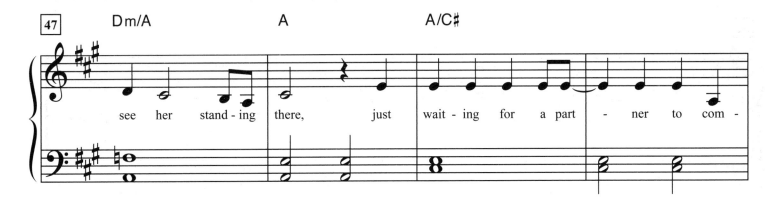

47 | **Dm/A** | **A** | **A/C#**

see her stand - ing there, just wait - ing for a part - ner to com -

51 | **D** | **F#m** | **D**

pose. And I wish my moth - er still could hear__ that

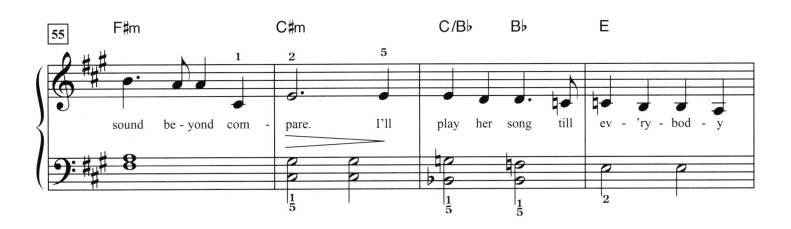

55 | **F#m** | **C#m** | **C/B♭** | **B♭** | **E**

sound be - yond com - pare. I'll play her song till ev - 'ry - bod - y

*Chorus:*

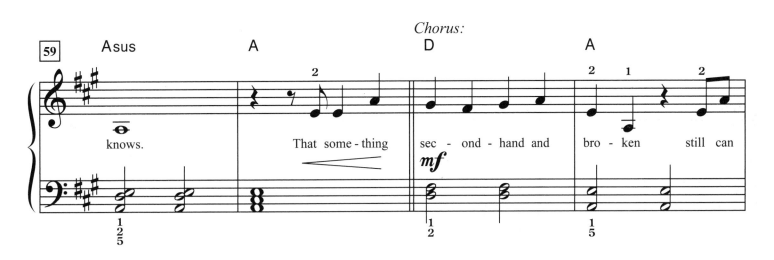

59 | **Asus** | **A** | **D** | **A**

knows. That some - thing sec - ond - hand and bro - ken still can

# THE STORY

Words and Music by
Phil Hanseroth
Arranged by Carol Matz

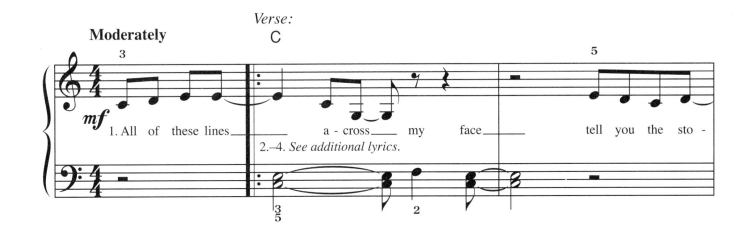

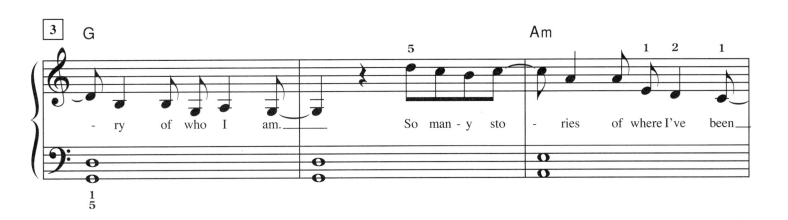

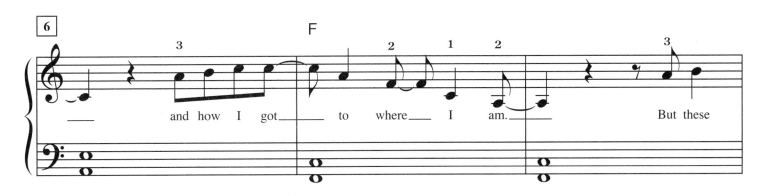

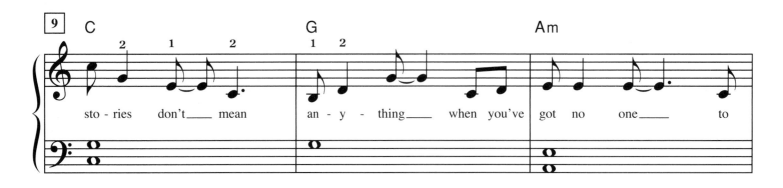

sto - ries don't___ mean an - y - thing___ when you've got no one___ to

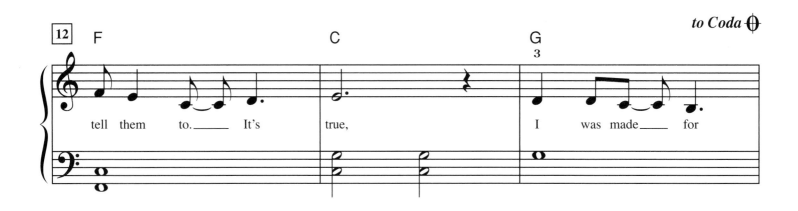

*to Coda*

tell them to.___ It's true, I was made___ for

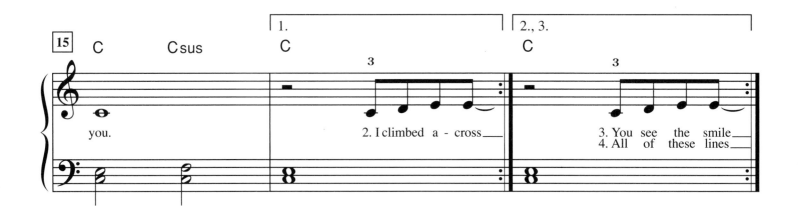

you.

1.
2. I climbed a - cross___

2., 3.
3. You see the smile___
4. All of these lines___

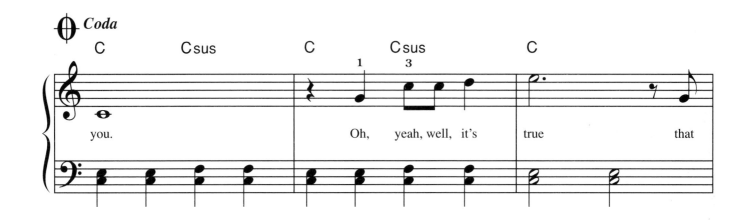

*Coda*

you. Oh, yeah, well, it's true that

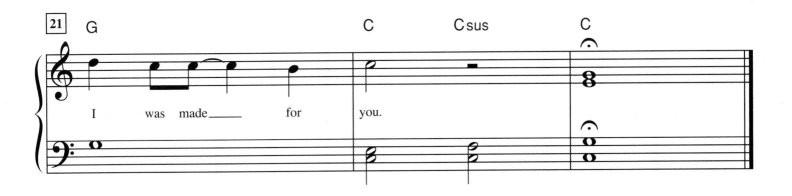

*Verse 2:*
I climbed across the mountain tops,
Swam all across the ocean blue.
I crossed all the lines, and I broke all the rules,
But, baby, I broke them all for you.
Oh, because even when I was flat broke,
You made me feel like a million bucks. You do.
I was made for you.


*Verse 3:*
You see the smile that's on my mouth?
It's hiding the words that don't come out.
All of my friends who think that I'm blessed,
They don't know my head is a mess.
No, they don't know who I really am.
And they don't know what I've been through like you do.
And I was made for you.


*Verse 4:*
All of these lines across my face
Tell you the story of who I am.
So many stories of where I've been
And how I got to where I am.
Oh, but these stories don't mean anything
When you've got no one to tell them to. It's true.
I was made for you.

# TONGUE TIED

Words and Music by
Christian Zucconi, Hannah Hooper, Andrew Wessen,
Sean Gadd and Ryan Rabin
Arranged by Carol Matz

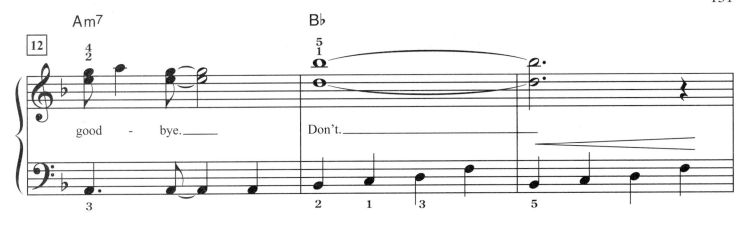

good - bye._____   Don't._____

**1.**

**2.**

Don't leave me tongue - tied.   Let's stay up all___ night.

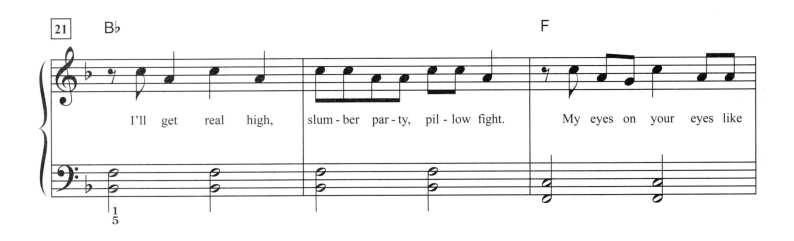

I'll get real high,   slum - ber par - ty,  pil - low fight.   My eyes on your eyes like

Pe - ter Pan up in the sky. My best friend's house to - night, let's bump the beats till bed - dy - bye.

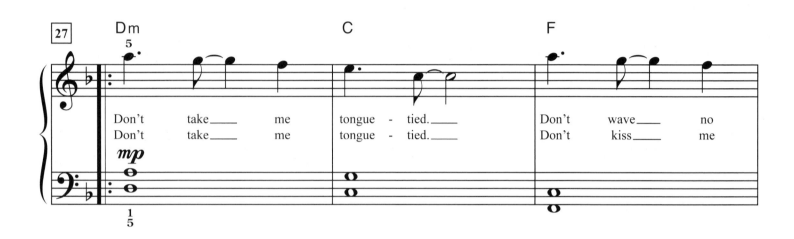

Don't take____ me tongue - tied.____ Don't wave____ no
Don't take____ me tongue - tied.____ Don't kiss____ me

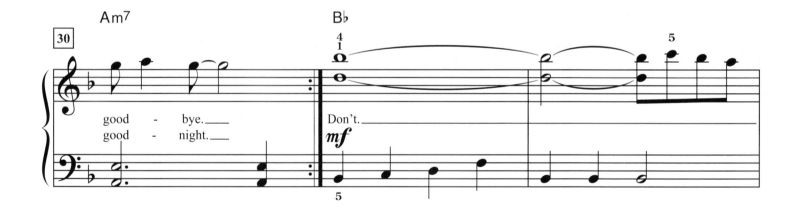

good - bye.____ Don't.____
good - night.____

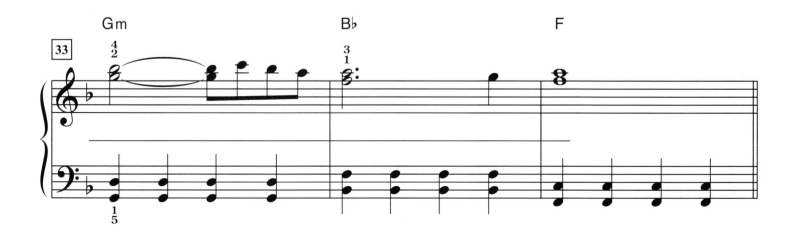

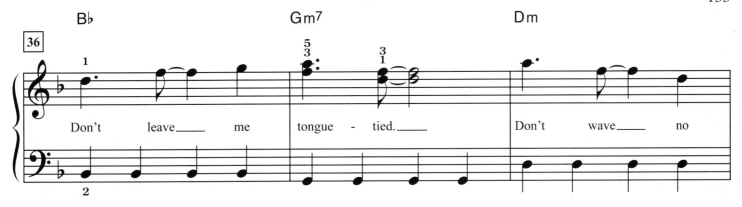

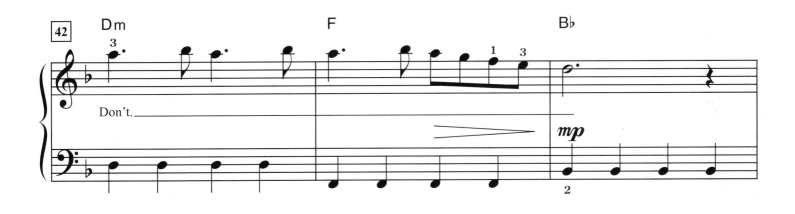

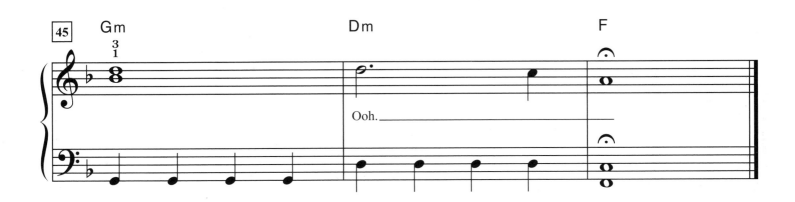

# WIDE AWAKE

Words and Music by
Katy Perry, Bonnie McKee, Lukasz Gottwald,
Max Martin and Henry Walter
Arranged by Carol Matz

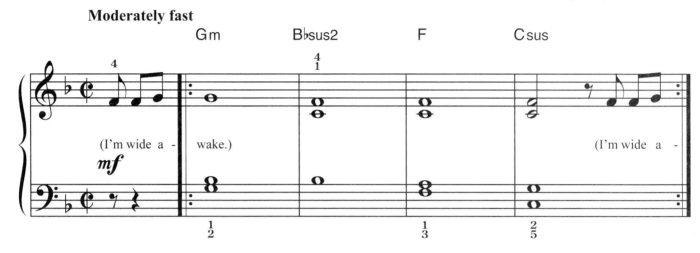

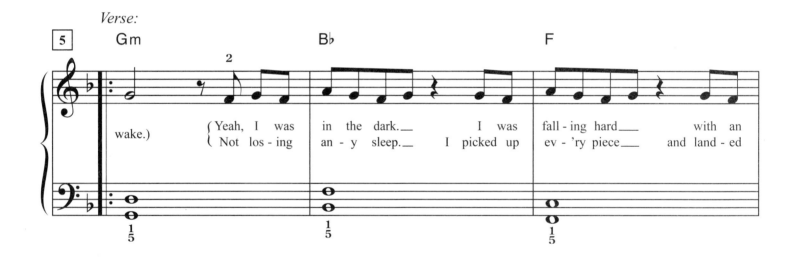

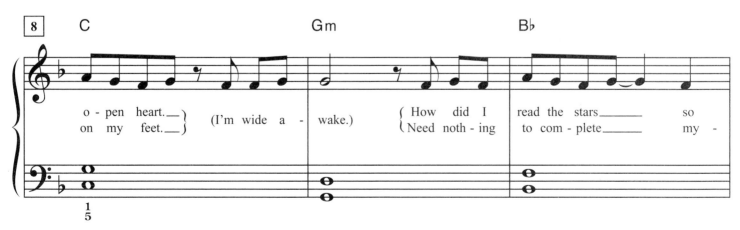

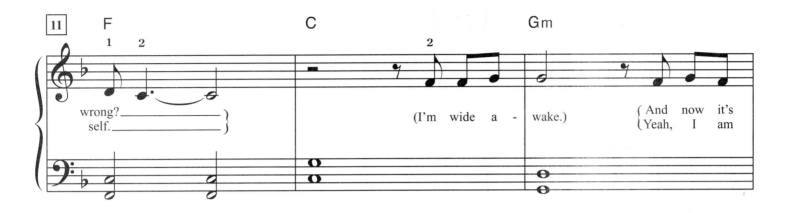

*Pre-Chorus:*

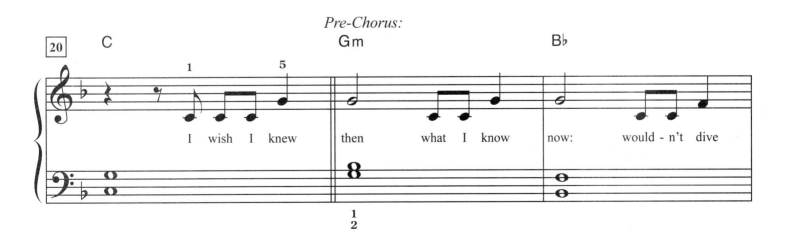

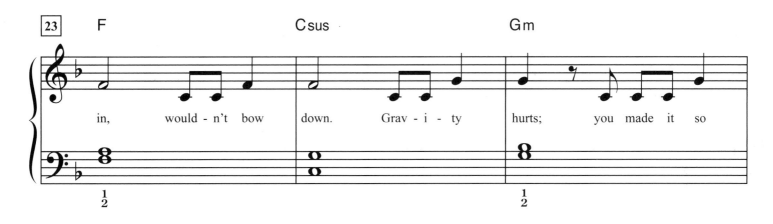

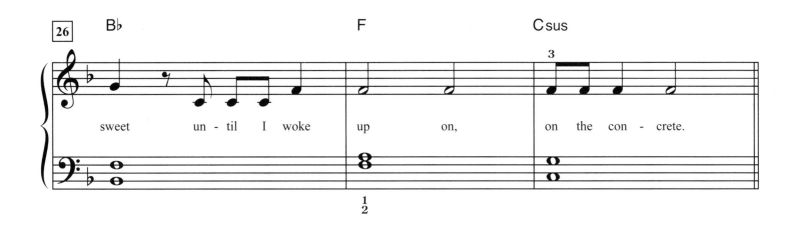

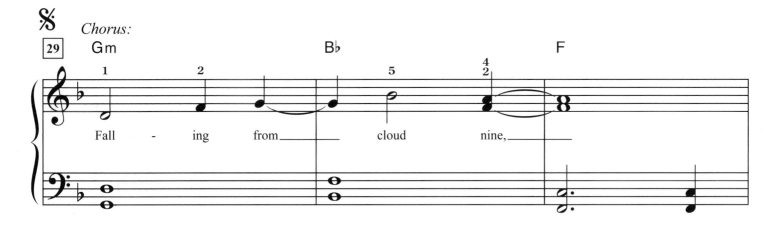

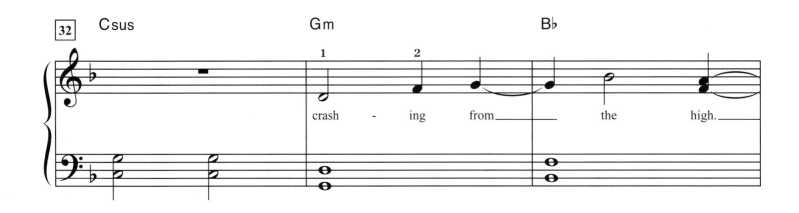

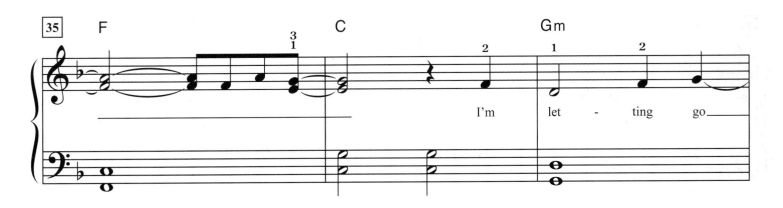

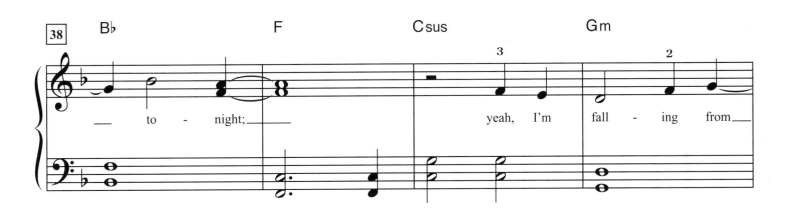

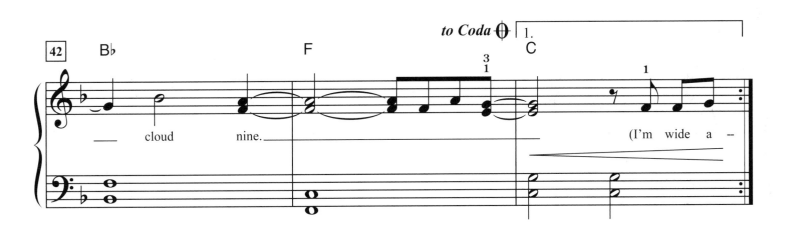

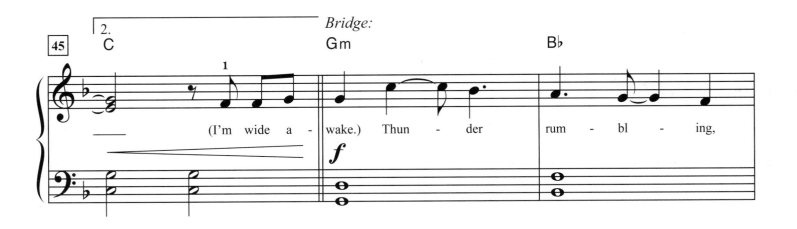

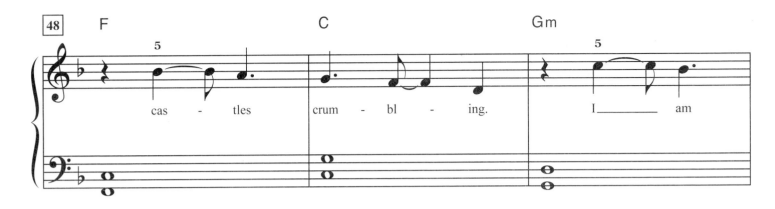

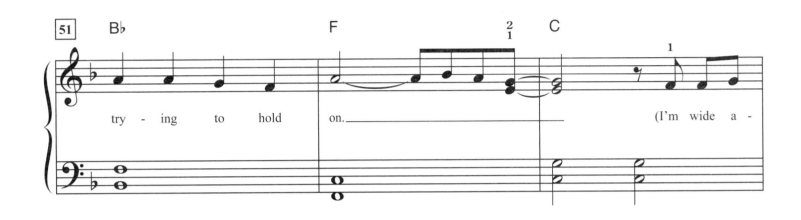

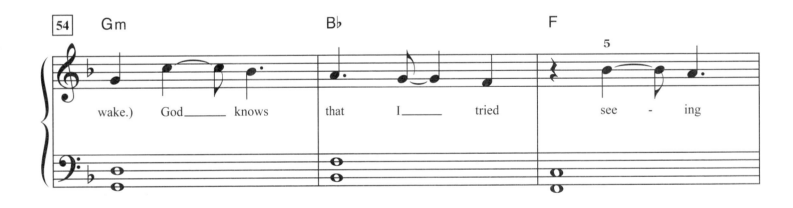

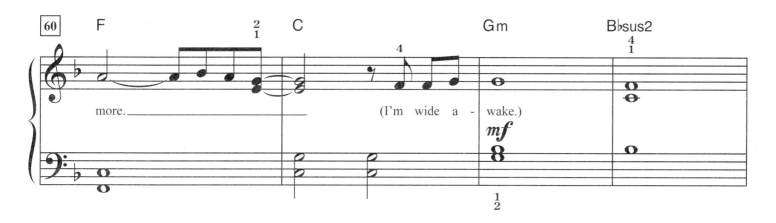

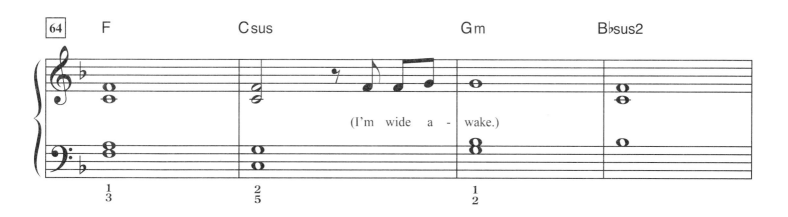

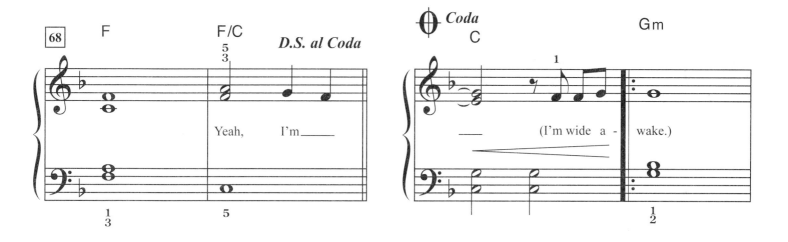

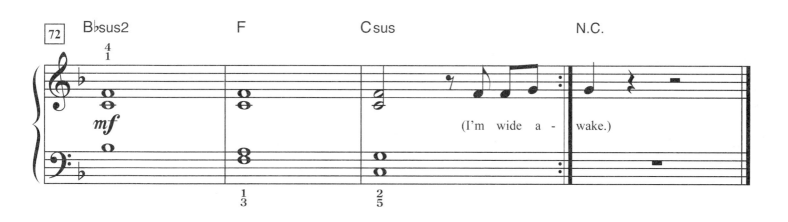

# WE ARE YOUNG

Words and Music by
Nate Ruess, Andrew Dost,
Jack Antonoff and Jeffrey Bhasker
Arranged by Carol Matz

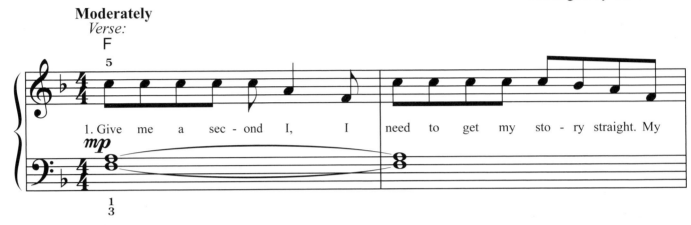

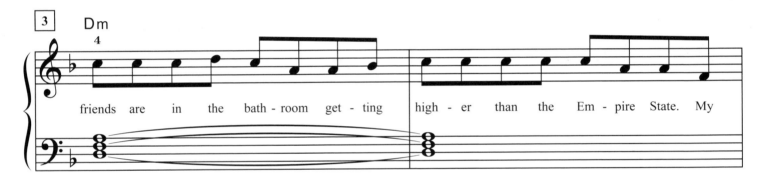

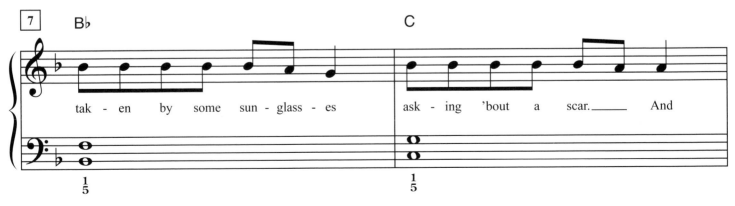

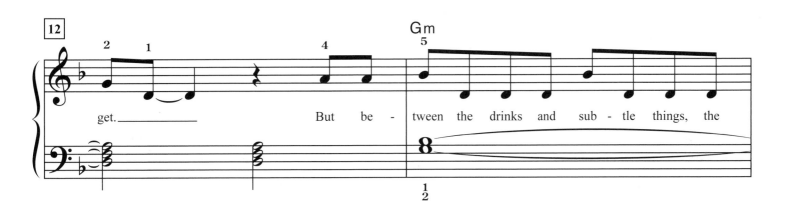

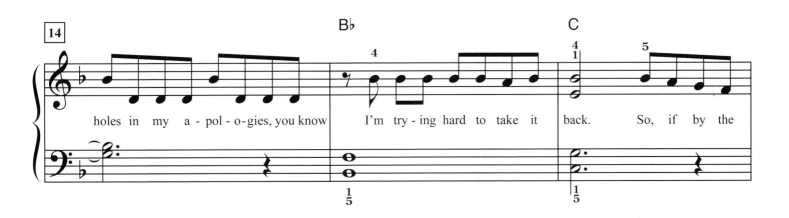

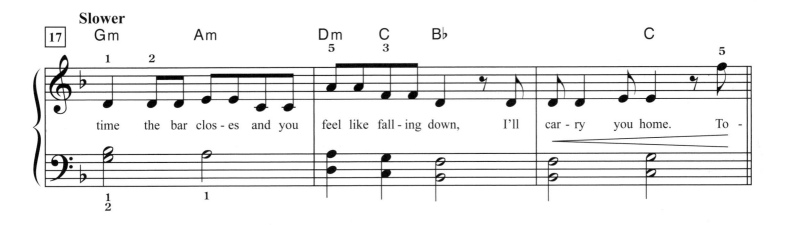

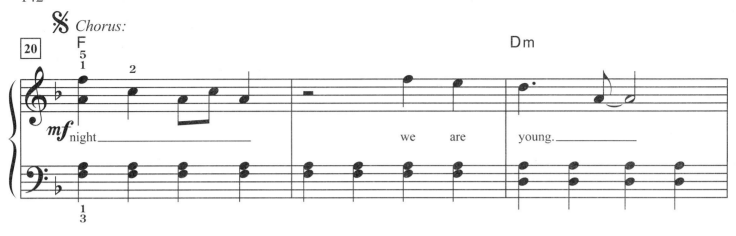

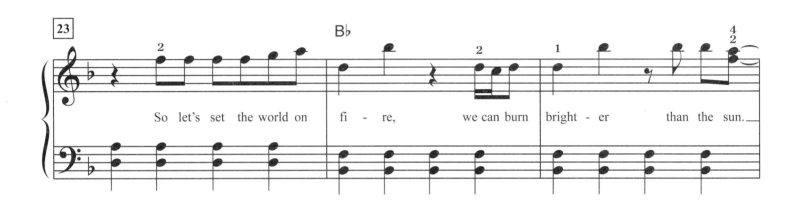

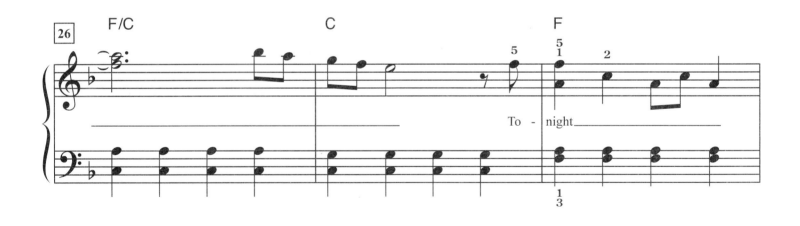

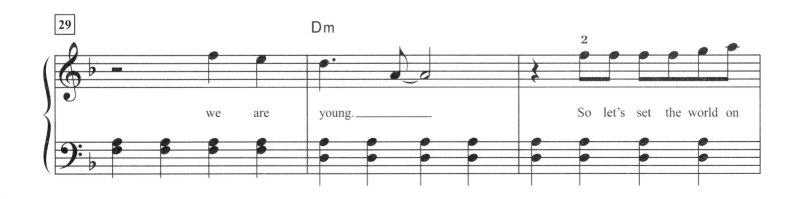

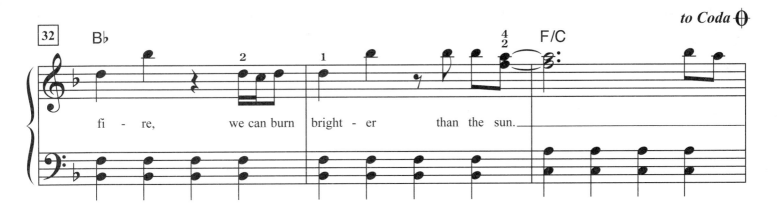

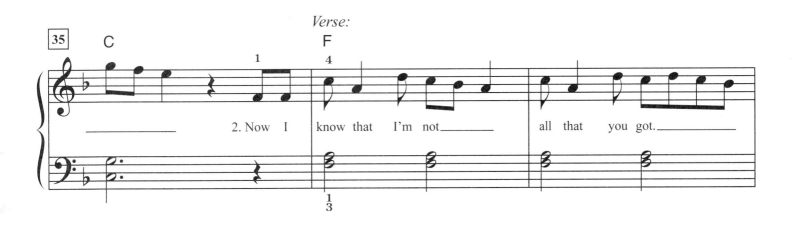

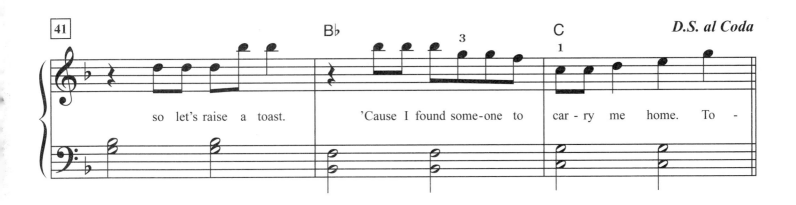

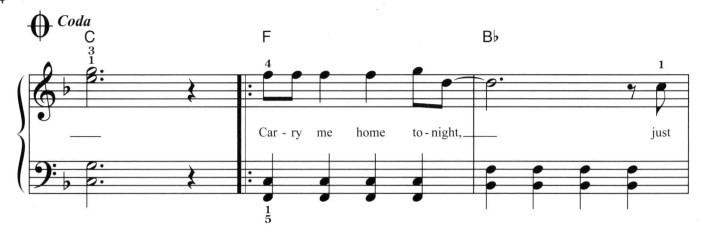

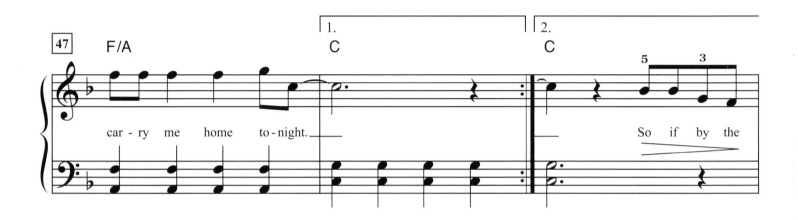

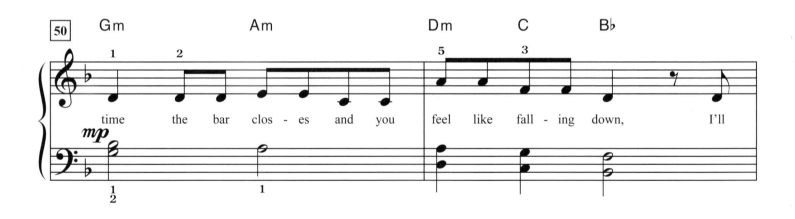

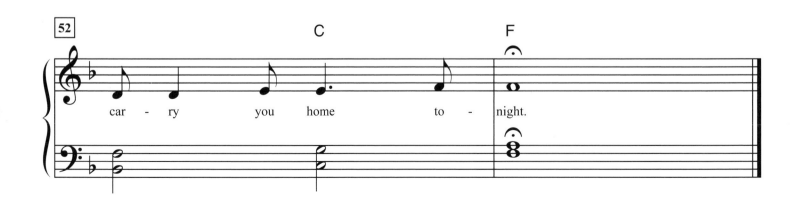